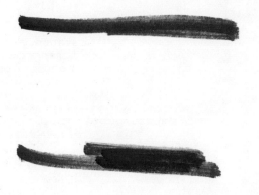

The Struggle Is the Message:

The Organization and Ideology of the Anti-War Movement

Books by Irving Louis Horowitz

THE STRUGGLE IS THE MESSAGE
PROFESSING SOCIOLOGY
THREE WORLDS OF DEVELOPMENT
REVOLUTION IN BRAZIL
THE WAR GAME
RADICALISM AND THE REVOLT AGAINST REASON
PHILOSOPHY, SCIENCE AND THE SOCIOLOGY OF KNOWLEDGE
THE IDEA OF WAR AND PEACE

Edited

MASSES IN LATIN AMERICA
CUBAN COMMUNISM
SOCIOLOGICAL SELF-IMAGES
LATIN AMERICAN RADICALISM
THE RISE AND FALL OF PROJECT CAMELOT
THE NEW SOCIOLOGY
THE ANARCHISTS
POWER, POLITICS AND PEOPLE
SOCIOLOGY AND PRAGMATISM
OUTLINES OF SOCIOLOGY
HISTORIA Y ELEMENTOS DE LA SOCIOLOGIA DEL CONOCIMIENTO

the
STRUGGLE
is the
MESSAGE:

the
Organization and Ideology
of the
Anti-War
Movement

IRVING LOUIS HOROWITZ

THE GLENDESSARY PRESS — BERKELEY

Consulting Editor:

Donald A. Hansen, *University of California, Berkeley*

To A. J. Muste, 1885-1967

CONTENTS

PREFACE

There is a relatively extensive literature on "violence in the streets" and on "urban violence" (or on nearly every phase of violence linked to the social and psychological behavior of the black American). There is, however, no corresponding systematic treatment of violence in the anti-war movement—despite the fact that the "war question" and the "black question" have emerged as the two central motifs in the political mosaic of the current decade. This study therefore represents a preliminary excursion into the connection between social movements and political organization.

When I was provided with the opportunity to help repair this break in the sociological literature, I naturally and enthusiastically accepted the challenge. The occasion was the formation of a special task force on violent aspects of protest and confrontation formed under the auspices of the National Commission on the Causes and Prevention of Violence. My own role as both an author of a study and a staff consultant to the special task force prevented the earlier publication of my work, since the overall findings obviously took precedence. However, now that these general findings have appeared in *The Politics of Protest*, the more specific aspects of the problem (and it might be added the more specu-lative aspects as well) can be made available to the interested public. It need only be added that any similarity between many of the observa-tions and findings (and graphs) found in the first part of the text here and in Chapter II of *The Politics of Protest* is *not* accidental. The materials gathered and published in that chapter were largely drawn from my report to the task force of the Commission. However, this is the first complete and unabridged version of my materials, and hope-fully the contents will be considered meritorious enough to warrant publication in this fashion.

In the course of work it proved easy to observe the parallels in the "natural history of violence." Here the insights of such classicists as LeBon, Freud, and Dewey, not to mention the contributions of modernists like Herbert Blumer, George Rude, and Kurt Lang, proved invaluable. It was much more difficult to explain the variations from such parallels once a careful examination was made of the documents and doings of the current anti-war movement in the United States. Therefore, although this essay is considerably longer than I would have liked it to be, the fact that little could be taken for granted, and so few aspects of the immediate problem referred to work done elsewhere, prevented me from exercising the virtue of brevity. I therefore request the reader's indulgence and understanding.

Since nowhere in the text do I make explicit my reasons for the choice of quasi-McLuhanisms for the title and part titles, it might be worthwhile to do so at the outset. "The struggle is the message" was selected for the first part because it conveys the three-fold aspect of the current anti-war movement with respect to violence. First is the conscious selection of the method of confrontation with authority, directly and in the field of combat, over the method of representation, through which select elites form a consensus through negotiation. Second, there is the widespread belief of the participants that the precise goals of the anti-war movement cannot be framed. In a sense, the end of any particular conflict, such as the Vietnam War, is no longer so primary an issue as that of conducting an assault on the "war system" itself. The very indeterminateness of foreign relations thus serves to add, to the burdens of membership in the anti-war movement, increased moralization of instrumentalities used as well as goals sought. Third, even vague and impersonal enemies like the middle or industrial classes have become further diffused to the point of loss, and this is clearly associated with the relative absence of focused aims of protest. The anti-war movement is thus more prone to violent response as a show of power than it might be if it had an ideology based on the supportive power of a major social class.

The "benefits" of participation in the movement are, in some definite sense, more linked to the act of participation and its psychological-therapeutic rewards for individuals than to any presumed long-range social rewards. It might be said that the current anti-war movement represents a revolt against the Protestant Ethic and its avoidance of violence which restrained earlier revolutionary movements in this country, and an assertion instead that participation in the movement is itself exciting and satisfies longings for personal importance.

In this way, a subtle shift takes place that transforms the struggle from an instrumentality (customarily associated with liberalism) to a fundamental aspiration (customarily associated with radicalism).

The chapters in the second part carry the theme of radicalism as an end of peace activities and peace action as a focus of attention for radicalism—"the message is the struggle." The initial chapter in this section is taken from a summary of a conference report delivered in February 1969 at the Center for the Study of Democratic Institutions in Santa Barbara. An earlier version was published in the *Center Magazine*. The second chapter of Part II was a paper first presented at a conference sponsored by the national office of the American Friends Service Committee in July 1962. At that time it was offered as a firm and yet friendly critique of the pacifist position. It also appeared in an earlier collection of papers of mine, *The War Game: Studies of the New Civilian Militarists.* Because of the timeliness of this paper, I decided to revise it thoroughly and offer it as an historical account, rather than a normative statement. The third chapter in this section is offered as a reflection on the radical impulses of the sixties in the United States, and how they compare and contrast with that remarkable *fin de siècle* epoch in France. It too appeared in an earlier version in the periodical *New Politics*. The chapter "From Teach-In to Moratorium" was a public statement issued for the two 1969 moratoriums. It was delivered first at Rutgers University in October, and then, in a revised version, at the Pennsylvania State University. Neither version was really suitable for permanent presentation, so this essay too has been considerably revised, despite its recent origins. I am grateful to the original publishers and sponsors of the material in the second part for kindly permitting this use.

I wish to acknowledge the assistance provided by Phyllis Malamud and Martin Liebowitz in helping to formulate problems and gather information. Their enthusiasm for this project was infectious, and their support truly invaluable. Adeline Sneider, who turned scribblings into text, could do so only because she is a thinker no less than a secretary.

A number of my colleagues were good enough to comment on and criticize my study. My thanks for such thankless work goes to Bennett M. Berger (University of California, Davis), Albert K. Cohen (University of California, Santa Cruz), Robert L. Hamblin (Washington University), Gary T. Marx (Harvard University), Sheldon L. Messinger (University of California, Berkeley), Charles C. Moskos, Jr. (Northwestern University), Lee Rainwater (Harvard University), Jerome H. Skolnick (University of Chicago), Roland L. Warren (Brandeis University), and Harvey Wheeler (Center for the Study of Democratic Institutions).

I have had the first-rate assistance of two fine secretaries, Margaret May and Gertrude LeGoff, and a fine copy editor, Mary Ellen Curtis. I also want to express my thanks to Danielle Salti for her fine indexing and fact checking—unheralded chores that make a big difference to author and reader alike. A special note of thanks is due to Professor

David Gold of the University of California at Santa Barbara. His urging that my Commission study be expanded and published, with his recommendation of the Glendessary Press, sparked me to organize my materials into this small book.

IRVING LOUIS HOROWITZ

Rutgers University
February 5, 1970

Part I

The Struggle Is the Message: The Liberal Pivot

THE PROBLEM

OF SOCIAL 1

CAUSATION

From four o'clock until after midnight the east side was the scene of the last desperate mob outbreaks. The streets became battle-grounds as newly arrived units of soldiers set up howitzers and fired time and time again into the assembled crowds, meanwhile advancing in solid ranks. Scores of rioters manned the rooftops, firing muskets and pistols and pelting the soldiers with bricks and missiles. The battle raged incessantly, the ever increasing rashness and desperation of the mob being met by active displays of force. Howitzers continually raked the streets, but toward midnight quiet was restored, though pillaging of stores and shops continued until dawn.

This vivid description, with the exception of the word "musket," could well be a wire service report on any American city with a large black ghetto. But this journalistic ethnography is nothing of the sort. It is instead a description of the New York City anti-draft riots, in July of 1863 (cf. Heaps, 1966:50-60; and Lader, 1959:44-49).

The poor people of New York, particularly the Irish (who

formed a quarter of the city's population), objected to the Civil War as "a rich man's war and a poor man's fight." This was underscored by the strange provision of the draft law which permitted a draftee to pay his local board $300 for his exemption or to replace himself with another potential soldier—who could even have been his slave. This practice was not encouraged, but was tolerated within limits. As Millis (1956) noted, this clearly favored the wealthy classes, since the average weekly laborer's wage at that time was $20.

But as is so characteristic in American history, the low level of political organization in the 1863 riots meant that the violence was random and diluted. The revolt of the poor was not directed particularly at the wealthy classes, but rather at the feared and hated blacks—who were viewed as the immediate cause of the Civil War. The crowds lacked direction or leadership, and what began as a spontaneous mass confrontation with the draft ended in sporadic, frustrated attacks on the blacks of New York City.

This historical illustration shows that militant anti-war movements (insofar as anti-war and anti-draft movements can be equated) may at times overlap with violent anti-black uprisings—but that relation is far from constant. It also points up the fact that anti-war struggles must be differentiated from pacifism: resistance to a particular war does not necessarily herald commitment to a general philosophy.

The purpose of this book is to analyze the relation between the contemporary anti-war movement and contemporary mass violence: specifically the connections, if any, between the United States military commitment in Vietnam and the rising tide of violent public resentment and dissatisfaction; the emergence of what might be called indigenous guerrilla violence as well as plain street violence. To begin, we must consider the several problems that complicate this analysis.

First, there is the problem of defining an anti-war movement or an anti-draft rally. Some rallies and demonstrations organized against the war shift their focus to related problems. For example, what begins as an anti-war demonstration may end up as an attack on the university administration, as has happened with any number of student rallies at the University of California. Protests often employ the war to highlight other problems—such demonstrations may have as their base the War on Poverty or the character of university contracts with private industries. The essential theme of many black protests against the war is that funds spent abroad could better be spent in the ghetto. Therefore, the very definition of anti-war movements is itself contestable.

Second, since many anti-war rallies and demonstrations do not generate violence, it is difficult to concede that protest necessarily leads to violence. Therefore, no significant correlation between protest and violence can be claimed.

Third, the degree of violence is not necessarily linked with the size of the demonstration. There can be high violence and low participation (as in the Chicago Convention demonstrations of August, 1968), or low violence and high participation (as in the New York Spring Mobilization of April, 1967). The issue of violence is linked far more to organization (or lack of it) than to sheer numbers.

Fourth, the investigator is confronted with the problem of determining interactional consequence. Violence merely as a quantum is rarely the question. Rather, it is *who* commits violence against whom, the rationale given for violence, and the degree of violence over and above that amount necessary to gain the stated objectives. The present relationship between the police or the National Guard and anti-war demonstrators is therefore extremely important, particularly since we are confronted not only with a statistical problem but also with interactions between those who instigate violence and those who claim to be violated.

Fifth, there is an area of problems involving operating norms, where stereotyped behavior may be mutually expected or even encouraged. Indeed, officials on each side may have a vested interest in fulfilling estimates and predictions, since future status in a demonstration or policing organization may turn on an official's capacity to claim prognostic ability. Police intelligence estimates typically predict that demonstrators will be unruly and uncooperative, while antiwar demonstration leaders anticipate police vindictiveness or physical aggression. Hence, it is by no means self-evident that increasing the ratio of police to demonstrators decreases the probability and the amount of violence. The data point in the other direction: high mobilization on both sides yields high violence. Thus the question of cause and effect, of who initiates violence and who responds, has to be resolved empirically, not a priori. Nor is this true for police and demonstrators only. Concepts of property rights and human rights, of what is to be defended, who actually owns the land on which demonstrations occur, the validity of permits, the duration of a protest—all involve debatable notions of law, and are not just spontaneous consequences of interaction.

These are the major parameters which, as a general rule, investigators have to come to terms with. The first five are spatial issues of correlation, definitions, and interactional consequence.

Sixth, there is the dimension of the explained variation of violence over time, i.e., the specific set of conflicts that a nation is involved in at a specific time and the organizational mechanisms available for political reconciliation of contending social forces.

Pervading all these factors is the consideration of duration:

of violent contact between the demonstrators and police on the one hand and of the war issue being demonstrated against on the other. Prolonged and repeated contact can, out of frustration or bitterness, lead to an escalation of violence. The longer disputants remain under the threat of violent contact, the more cause they give each other for violence, and the less likely does opposition seem to be legitimate. In relation to the present Vietnam conflict, the longer the government pursues war action that lacks clear norms and legitimate public presentation, and the greater the failure of tactics intended to achieve victory, the more public demonstrations will be associated with violence. As the war escalates, or even continues at a high level of conflict, national frustration rises. As this occurs, anti-war sentiment increases and militancy escalates within the organized anti-war movement.

Anti-war demonstrations and violence are directly related to specific world events. Wars of greater magnitude than the Vietnam War have provoked little popular resistance. World War II was a widely accepted, if not popular, war, and the Korean War was at least neutrally received. Popular violence is related to the degree that the polity, and especially draft age youth, accept political policy as legitimate. Accordingly, when warfare has become legitimate in the eye of the public, when a given conflict has a binding value on the total population, the anti-war movement tends to be small.

New tactics introduced to meet the failures of previous tactics in a non-legitimized war expand conflict. Concurrently, tactical availabilities for effective public opposition are exhausted. Hence, the push to violence is as much a function of the exhaustion of non-violent possibilities in resolving the war problem as it is a declared intent of the anti-war protest movement.

RALLIES

2 IN SEARCH

OF STRATEGIES

This chapter provides a qualitative analysis of data from rallies and demonstrations through the years 1965 to 1968 (see Appendix). One of the most striking features of the data is that the number of rallies, protests, and demonstrations increases steadily from 1965 through 1967, while in 1968 it tapers off as anti-war protest becomes enmeshed in the mobilization for presidential politics. The demonstrations held in 1968, however, were almost always large, and they engendered the sharpest confrontations of demonstrators and law enforcement officials (vividly illustrated by the demonstrations accompanying the Democratic Convention held in Chicago).

This tends to verify the contention that as the level of political organization and sophistication increases, there are three consequences: (1) the numbers of rallies and demonstrations taper off considerably; (2) the size and scope of those that are held sharply increase; (3) higher organization yields lesser amounts of violence. These propositions will be discussed more extensively later in the chapter.

In 1965, the anti-war movement wanted "dialogue" rather than "confrontation." Leadership by such traditionalist organizations as the American Friends Service Committee and Committee for a Sane Nuclear Policy gave it the impulse for participation in at least the outer perimeters of governmental power. Teach-ins and government "truth teams" to debate national unity, seminars at Airlie House between peace leaders and sympathetic Congressmen, forums involving members of the Institute for Policy Studies and federal bureaucrats, and, in general, contacts between organizations like Women Strike for Peace and United Nations representatives remained the key focal points for dramatizing anti-war sentiments. Even the pacifist Committee for Nonviolent Action, willing to commit civil disobedience, asked for and received permission to roam through the corridors of the Pentagon to hand out pamphlets and meet with Secretary of Defense McNamara.

While these tactics remain a factor in the current anti-war movement, they occur under a larger umbrella of direct-action techniques sponsored by a more militant leadership than these groups were willing to accept a few short years ago.* The tactics of specialized centers of organizational power, each existentially "doing its own thing," has thus allowed the peace movement to grow without the customary factionalism traditional of anti-war groupings in the United States.†

* Some of these traditionalist organizations have also become more militant. For example, Benjamin Spock resigned as national co-chairman of SANE to become co-chairman of the National Conference for a New Politics, on October 2, 1967. He was then quoted as saying: "More militancy is needed, both in the black liberation movement and the peace movement."

† This does not mean that the current peace movement has been entirely free of factionalism. In November of 1965, for instance, the New York Committee to End the War in Vietnam disbanded because of strategic differences between the Socialist Workers Party and Students for a Democratic Society. While SDS sought a more broadly based movement, the Trotskyite SWP wanted one that declared the war illegal.

Tracing rallies and demonstrations from 1965 to 1968 shows that the tactics used in California were more radical at a much earlier time than those of demonstrations elsewhere. Perhaps the polarization of political forces occurred sooner in California than elsewhere. In any event, rallies there set the tone and the pace for the message of struggle throughout the rest of the nation. Oakland is a particularly revealing case. As early as 1965 disruption was employed as a major tactic, including the stopping of troop trains. Such overt disruption by the peace movement elsewhere did not become common until 1967.

The "direct action" tactics of the anti-war movement first became noticeable late in 1965. Protest became the order of the day as the escalation of the Vietnam War mounted. Confrontation in the form of silent days of protest, draft card burnings, and even symbolic suicides (self-immolation by Norman Morrison, Alice Herz, and Roger Laporte) were employed with considerable effect. Simulation of Gandhian tactics of civil disobedience, with the detention of troop trains in Oakland and the picketing of draft stations, also began in 1965. But according to a key figure in the anti-war movement, Staughton Lynd (1968a: 314-322), even this stepped-up set of actions was inadequate to the task at hand. "We were too little committed to direct action, not too much."

Confrontation accelerated in 1966, and not just in size. Indeed, the typical demonstration shifted from mass participation to direct action (such as draft card burning) by the few, while the larger crowd stood by as "sympathetic witnesses." But even this was lacking in specificity. As Lynd indicates: "The most obvious and tragic failure of the movement this last year [1965] has been its failure to develop a responsible program against the draft. We have succeeded in stimulating debate in Congress, but we have left millions of young men, one by one struggling with the desperate and frightening question, to fend for themselves." Thus, strategic changes during 1966 included a sharper focus on the anti-draft movement. Protests against taking Selective Service examinations, assistance in getting thermonuclear pacifists out of the country, attacks on those university administrations issuing class rankings for recruitment purposes, and even harassment and badgering of public officials involved with Selective Service, all became important features of the movement.

Throughout 1966 answers were attempted to the question that plagued the peace movement, namely, appropriate levels of response. The major dilemma of anti-war movement activities in the recent past was lack of concreteness, lack of specific direction in response to the state. The struggle around the black issue was concrete. It involved boycotts and open housing ordinances, and it was much more flexible in that the goals of black protest were more easily defined and definable, especially in the South. Only within the last three years have the tactics of the peace movement become adjusted to the specifics of the war as such. Direct confrontation with draft boards and even the beginning of acts of sabotage against ROTC facilities indicate that political pragmatism has finally reached the anti-war movement. The violence of the anti-war movement is not so much a sensory experience as a pragmatic urgency to make specific the militant aims of the anti-war movement. Physical objects—buildings and ROTC encampments—thus helped portray the specific nature of the anti-war response to this specific Vietnam issue.

In 1967 militant tactics included protest against Dow Chemicals and other campus recruiters for what Kenneth Boulding calls the World War III industries. Protests occurred on campuses against Marine, Army, and Navy recruiters. Tactics also included disruption of the recruitment process per se. Disrupting induction, burning draft cards, defacing and ransacking files, all make it difficult for the military establishment to conduct its daily business. At least it makes such business more costly financially and emotionally. On the other hand, it also creates a strong conservative reaction to the peace movement both from civil and military sources.

The anti-war movement can be considered as an ideology in search of a tactic. And by 1967 the search took on the aura of desperate pragmatism, reflected in the first conversation between Norman Mailer (1968) and his fellow writer and political activist Mitchell Goodman concerning the March to Washington in October, 1967. The disillusionment was obvious.

> Goodman had just finished telling Mailer that there was going to be a March on Washington in about a month, and Mailer had hardly finished saying he doubted if he would attend since he had no desire to stand in a large meadow and listen to other men make speeches (Mailer was still furious at SANE for an occasion two years ago when the latter had wanted $50 in contribution from him for a protest in Washington, but did not think enough —or were too dismayed—of the text of a speech he had given in Berkeley about the war in Vietnam to invite him to speak); so he did not think he would go to Washington.

But Goodman was not to be denied. He asked whether Mailer had seen the circular sent around by the Mobilization Committee, and when assured he, Mailer, had not seen it, Goodman went on to say that the Washington Rally would be different. "Well, this one is a departure. Some of us are going to try to invade the corridors of the Pentagon during office hours and close down some of their operation." The group that Goodman represented, Resist, was also going to demonstrate at the Department of Justice in honor of students who turned in their draft cards. Mailer's subsequent participation is literary history, no less than real history. And while this is not the place to delve into the new tactics of the anti-war movement, certain very important items emerged from this new stage in the anti-war struggles.

(1) The anti-war movement did in fact escalate its tactics,

including those that would bring about a confrontation with the authorities.

(2) The basic tactical change was a changed attitude toward private property, or the inviolability of "property rights" over and against "human rights."

(3) At no point did the majority sector, even the extreme radical wings, publicly discuss, or resort to, initiating violence. Indeed, the movement went to considerable lengths to distinguish assaults on property from assaults on persons.

(4) The police, acting on the medieval juridical premise that property is the extension of the personal owner thereof, and thus he who attacks property is assaulting the person, made no distinction between property and person. In this way, the question of violence in the anti-war movement became a central focus of debate.

It is conceivable that at a later stage the anti-war movement might initiate violence in the form of guerrilla insurgency to gain some of its ends. There is scattered evidence that such a stage has been reached. But the strong pacifist bias of the anti-war movement, with its entrenched middle-class and student character, represents a group that probably contains the least number of people capable even of wielding weapons effectively, much less committed to violent confrontation with police or paramilitary units.

The available data compellingly suggest that the quantity of civil disobedience might be an indication of the growing disparity between what the police construe to be problems of maintaining law and order and the actual politicizing of the anti-war movement. As anti-war protests move increasingly into the political arena, with political "respectables" themselves announcing their opposition to the war, the forces of law and order continue to deal with anti-war protesters in traditional terms of deviance. This in itself may be sufficient to convert the anti-war movement into more militant, activist channels.

One outgrowth of the steady increase in the size of the anti-war movement is that demonstrator tactics become more violent as they are met with an unresponsive and hostile political system. The tactics move from orderly demonstrations and picket lines to petitions signed in blood and to protesters prepared for violence by showing up in motorcycle and football helmets, shouting insults at police. The following description of the 1968 Berkeley Independence Day Riots is indicative of this new mood of militant confrontation.

> What on Friday had been a violent confrontation became on Saturday a full-scale riot. The frightened and non-violent among the [Telegraph] Avenue community had prudently stayed home. As soon as demonstrators were able to regroup, police and police vehicles were greeted with barrages of stones and bottles. A modern plastic apartment building under construction a block away was set ablaze. The crowd selected its targets, concentrating on the Avenue stores whose owners had been particularly unsympathetic in the past and on those institutions which it considered symbolic of the repressive society. Rocks and bricks crashed through the windows of Bank of America and Wells Fargo branches. "Friendly" merchants were generally spared. (The Avenue's favorite bookstore, Cody's, suffered a broken window, but this was apparently an accident.) A nearby house, recently expropriated by the University, was set aflame. (Chain, 1968: 24.)

The expectancy of violence tends to reinforce the police in their own normative behavior. The very act of coming prepared for violence in a quasi-military confrontation can stimulate precisely the violent definition of the situation. In short, violence may be "spontaneous" in the immediate sense of who gets injured or the extent of fighting, but quite "deterministic" in the wider context.

The anti-war movement has escalated not only in terms of

violence, but perhaps more significantly, in a denial of legitimacy to the war in Vietnam as such. The annual Report of the Director of Selective Service indicates a geometric progression in the number of appeals considered by all state appeals boards in recent years. 1965 saw 9,741 appeals. 1966 saw 49,718. And in 1967 there were 119,167. The same situation exists with respect to direct appeals to Presidential authority for release from military duty.

As the anti-draft mood increased, the tactics of the anti-war movement changed drastically. Many leaders stated that the anti-war movement would from now on seek confrontation. This sentiment was frankly expressed by David Dellinger only a few days before the Pentagon March. As described brilliantly by Norman Mailer, the Pentagon March was a demarcation point. Violent action by police and National Guardsmen not only occurred, but from then on was expected. Confrontation replaced peaceful parades. Several weeks after the Pentagon March, the trend toward violence was confirmed. Police and picketers of Secretary Rusk clashed, after police restricted the numbers of picketers and a small minority of protesters provoked the police by stopping traffic and hurling plastic bags of cattle blood, stones, bricks, and bottles. Some of these tactics had been expected. The director of the Fifth Avenue Peace Parade Committee conceded that the coalition had permitted some resistance activities: "We were in agreement that demonstrations must be conducted on all levels. . . . Provo-type actions are necessary to obstruct the functioning of the War Machine" (Dellinger, 1967). However, police restrictions on the picketers had, he said, provoked more civil disobedience than planned.

By April 1968 the peace movement served notice that it would no longer obligingly cooperate with the authorities. David Dellinger threatened that the Mobilization Committee would not apply for a parade permit for its April 27 march. (It did, but when a dissident group did not, a bloody riot ensued.) "It would be a mistake to think that the fight against the war can be won in the ballot box," Dellinger (1968) said. "It still has to be won on the streets." He therefore suggested that any organization, so long as it had a fundamental commitment to anti-war protest, be allowed in the New York rally "to do its own thing." Doing one's "own thing" could be non-violent action, anticipation of violent action, provocation of police action by jeers and taunts or even the initiation of violence.

Another tactical change occurred in late 1967. Earlier rallies tended to be highly centralized, with orders issued from the top down. The later rallies increasingly tended to be decentralized, relying more on spontaneity from below. This may be the result of the changing ideology and organization of the peace movement—towards anarchism. The increased role of organizations like SDS, where not only confrontation but autonomy and localized action are important, also helped to blow the lid off anti-war protests.

The April 1968 rally is a case study in decentralization. In New York alone, there were several marches. The major rally was held in Sheep Meadow, while a minor but violent one was led by dissident leftist groups in Washington Square Park. For those in Washington Square decentralization was a tactic to confuse the police. Unlike the pacifist marches of the late fifties, the purpose was not to let the police know where they were going, and to keep a fully mobilized police force on its toes at all times. In previous years most anti-war demonstrators had cooperated with authorities by seeking a permit. In April, 1968, the rally cry "the streets belong to the people" became a major slogan, a clear spinoff from the student cry that "the universities belong to the students."

From late 1967 to 1968 new tactics were used because both police and judicial agencies had already become experienced with violence in the Civil Rights Movement. The accumulation of experience between the two movements set up a situation where the police responded indiscriminately. All demonstrators became deviant hippies and revolutionaries; in this sense all were "niggers." This escalated the propensity to undifferentiated response. The police were no longer able to distinguish between orderly demonstrations and any other kind. It seemed to them that property values themselves were being menaced by the politicalized "street scene." And demonstrators became less concerned with orderliness as a public value. Any demonstration in late 1967 and 1968 could be interpreted by the police as having a high potential for disorder, and often was dealt with accordingly.

Local history is an important criterion in mass violence. The Anti-War Rally of April 27 was violent. But one should bear in mind that the Columbia University Student Rebellion had erupted a few days earlier, and served as a model. The Poor People's Campaign was also about to start. The talk of violence in the media, no less than the deterioration of confidence in the "system," went together. The fact that it was Loyalty Day, when patriotism is paramount, undoubtedly contributed to police violence.

THE ORGANIZATION

3 AND IDEOLOGY

OF THE ANTI-WAR MOVEMENT

The organizational basis of the current anti-war movement is profoundly non-totalitarian and self-consciously anti-Stalinist. In this special sense, the critics are correct in calling the movement "anarchistic." Party doctrine in which, as Martov facetiously pointed out, "the Party is divided into those who sit and those who are sat upon," no longer exists. Local control is central. And just as individuals are encouraged to "do their thing," organizations are likewise exhorted to "do theirs" as well. This marks a self-conscious return to the American anarchist tradition, particularly its transcendentalist wing from Thoreau to Lysander Spooner.

The anti-war movement is no longer confined to totalitarian models derived from the thirties, when both the extreme Right and Left were tied to the ideological and functional needs of foreign powers such as Nazi Germany and Stalinist Russia; it has been able to extricate itself wholly from both Spenglerian and Marxian forms of historicism. "Laws of history" (which have always implied the serious study of social background) have given way to the

"Will of the People" (which always implies the resentment by activists against those who take history too seriously). The availability of successful foreign models of revolutionary change which have been "stage jumping" in character—such as the Soviet Union, China, and Cuba—precisely reinforce the trends toward domestic anarchism in the current anti-war movement. Thus, while it is important to appreciate the degree to which the anti-totalitarian qualities of the current anti-war movement have spilled over into an anti-rationalistic bias, it is no less important to recognize the intense moral concern the movement represents.

Nor is this merely an ideological choice. At the level of practice what is involved is the willingness to use, even the insistence upon using, direct action, irrespective of the chance for immediate political success. This is one key reason why exhortations to be reasonable and judicious are met with opposition. Rationality, whether in the form of American pragmatism or European historicism, is viewed as characterizing the "Old Left." What has occurred is a replication of the traditional problem within the Left between advocates of action and advocates of determinism. This is clearly the moment when the "triumph of the Will" seems to be in ascendance over the "laws of history." These abstract, indeed obtruse, considerations are well illustrated in the structure of the demonstrations at the Chicago Nominating Convention of the Democratic Party, held August 25 through 29, 1968. The general call went out through the National Mobilization Committee to End the War in Vietnam. The national chairman was David Dellinger and the leading Committee coordinator was Rennie Davis. But in fact, this "parent" organization was a coalition of more than one hundred anti-war, radical, and community groupings. Among these nuclear centers were such diverse organizations as Students for a Democratic Society, People Against Racism, Veterans for Peace, Clergy and Laymen Concerned about Vietnam Committee, and Women

Strike for Peace. These, called "movement centers," were united by the willingness to act, rather than by a common set of political values.

FIGURE 1: SIZE OF ANTI-WAR DEMONSTRATIONS
AND PERCENTAGE OF ANTI-WAR SENTIMENT

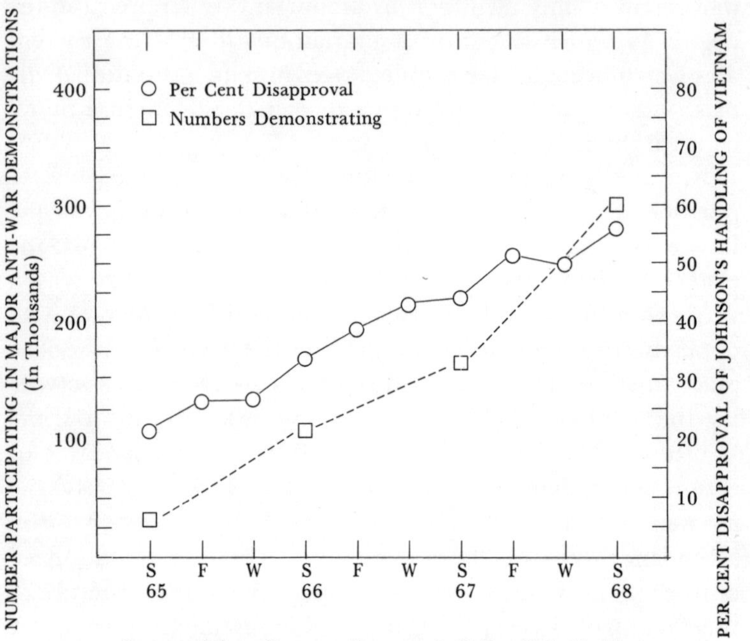

Source of data: Per cent disapproval, Gallup Poll; Number of participants in anti-war demonstrations involving 1000 or more persons, *New York Times Index* and *Facts on File.*
Code: S= Spring; F= Fall; W= Winter

Figure 1 offers graphic representation that the size of the anti-war demonstrations correlates precisely with a growing disaffection from the Vietnam War policies during the 1965-68 period. Given the fact that demonstrations in most parts of the country are "seasonal," the peak period for each year (spring) was computed, and then correlated with Gallup Poll data on support or opposition to the war policies of the Johnson administration. Two major conclusions follow: the anti-war movement as such is a main-line rather than a marginal activity, and its legitimacy derives from the general polarization of American attitudes and sentiments toward the war. This does not necessarily imply that violence in the anti-war movement bears the same correlation to the size of the protest movement, since violence for the most part is confined to a minuscule fraction of the anti-war movement.

A case could be made that the non-violent anti-war movement reached its peak point of success in the decision of President Johnson not to run for the presidency in 1968. It could also be said that the "clout" of the legitimate anti-war movement was restricted to a negative impact. Able to express its resentment for orthodox American foreign policy, it could not mobilize sufficient political power to galvanize either of the major parties at the national ticket level. Only after this became clear did the ultra-militant sector of the anti-war movement generate sufficient force to move matters into a violent assault on property and the draft system. This underscores the connection between violence and illegitimacy, and non-violence and legitimacy. Insofar as the legitimacy of protest remained unchallenged, the levels of violence were insignificant. But when such protest was unable to register political support, the "movement" took over from the "youth army" supporting the candidacies of Eugene McCarthy and Robert F. Kennedy.

The dilemma with the "movement centers" is that in exchange for maximizing spontaneous activity and autonomic political behavior, they also permit, or indeed almost make inevitable, a higher degree of violence than is the case for the older leftist control from the top down. Since a great many of the movement centers are comprised of militant groups, their demeanor in crisis situations, such as those that arose in

Chicago during the convention, tends to embrace the entire phalanx of resisters, including the pacifist-oriented groupings. The indiscriminate response of the police to threats to their social control of a situation only reinforces the schisms within the peace movement between traditional pacifists and politicalized radicals.

The problems are particularly acute for those portions of the anti-war movement dedicated to non-violent methods, and equally acute for those sectors of the police who might prefer the use of more confined and moderate treatment of anti-war demonstrators. It is not that the militant wing of the New Left should be prevented from pursuing its own tactics, but rather that in this very endeavor it tends to overwhelm more pacifist-inclined elements. Ironically, this same situation is reported with respect to police and National Guard behavior. In every demonstration there is a small cadre of officers who appear ready, and a large body of policemen who appear reluctant to engage in direct confrontation either with fists or with billy-clubs, Mace, or other weapons of limited destruction (cf. Kifner, 1968). The agony of the situation is that, while pacifists and policemen deny the existence of such tactical and even principled cleavages, neither side is remotely willing to isolate the precise source of violence. To do so would yield an impression of internal dissensions and "fink"-like behavior. Thus, the problem of personality and social structure remains, without hope of easy solution.

Not only were the anti-war protesters violent in their tactics. As a corollary, the counterdemonstrators, who were largely quiescent in earlier years, have also become more violent. Most counterdemonstrators earlier had heckled the anti-war protesters, taunting them with "Communist" or "pinko" as well as earthier derogatory terms. Some had thrown eggs or tomatoes at the demonstrators. In April, the counterdemonstrators, seemingly less organized than any of of the anti-war groups, started tearing down signs set up by the war protesters, breaking through lines, and trying to start fist fights.

The significant point is that the escalation of the Vietnam War has been matched by the escalation in anti-war protest actions. A certain Europeanization of populist politics has set in. This involves a sharp condemnation of orthodox parliamentarian politics as such and moves, inexorably, into a framework in which direct confrontation becomes the supreme test of worth. This might be considered the middle-class adaptation of the *foco* in guerrilla struggles, in which the will of the people is asserted through the participants at specific points of struggle. A *fin de siècle* phenomenon reappears: the goals of the struggle become fluid, indefinite, and even suspect, while the forms of struggle become sharper and consuming. In the America of today as in the France of 1898 the struggle is the message.

THE CHANGING FOCUS

4   OF ANTI-WAR

ORGANIZATION

Anti-war organization is an amorphous, almost amoeba-like phenomenon. But insofar as there is any clear pattern of development in the organizational structure of the anti-war movement in the United States, it may be said to have emerged in three stages—each within the marginal context of radical politics. First, covering a period roughly between 1952 and 1956, there was a discernible ideological thawing out of the communist-oriented Left. Out of the ashes of the McCarthy assault on the feeble American communist organization, and out of a corresponding period of "thaw" in the Soviet Union and its loosening effects upon communists everywhere, there emerged left-wing efforts at ideological independence and more democratic organizational procedures. The second period, between 1957 and 1965, involved the rebirth of issue-oriented leftism. In this period new radical groups were formed which were primarily involved in the struggle for the rights of blacks: on the educational, economic, and political levels.

For the pacifist wing, this second stage was characterized by a touching faith in the rationality of all men and in individual, dramaturgical acts: individuals sailing into the Pacific Ocean atom bomb test areas (sponsored by the Committee of Nonviolent Action—CNVA—which was founded in 1957); Quaker demonstrations against land-launched missiles in Omaha, Nebraska; and various lengthy cross-national "walks for peace" (cf. Lynd, 1966: 310-376).

But by 1965 several major events took place. On the one hand, there was the growing nationalization of black radicalism which took on separatist overtones and sought exclusively black leadership. On the other hand, the United States' involvement in Vietnam led to her becoming a party to war, a fact which became dramatically real for the American population in 1965. Now the white radical movement had its ready-made ideological issue. This third period was first discerned late in 1964 after the student revolt at Berkeley which injected into the radical mainstream a student militancy for university and, finally, social reform on a broad scale. Thus an initial left-wing thaw issued into the radical pluralism of blacks, students, and sympathetic liberal professionals.

The first major anti-war strategy following the escalation of the Vietnam War early in 1965 was that of the teach-in. It reflected not only an urge to "dialogue," but carried the implicit threat that the American university system would be converted into a politically relevant complex as an answer to the war. The intelligentsia in the United States, which in all past wars of the century was solidly behind the pro-war consensus, this time made a decisive break with its own tradition. Yet, the genteel nature of the resistance to war followed closely the general pacifist response which was still dominant. The uses of reason were sure to triumph over the forces of might (cf. Menashe and Radosh, 1967). It is not that the teach-in concept has been totally abandoned, but rather, as in the March on the Pentagon, it was fused to active resistance and massive disruption (cf. Dellinger, 1967b: 4-5).

If the black nationalist movement was cutting its ties from the orthodox white liberal anti-war supports, the same was not true in reverse. For the number of blacks involved in anti-war protest movements have most often come from the upper leadership level of the black protest movement, while whites, sensing the vitality the black movement holds for radicalism as such, have consistently sought to attach themselves to civil rights struggles. It is this white attachment to black protest which has maintained tactical resemblances between the anti-war movement and the black liberation movement and has encouraged overlapping memberships and actions. In fact, the present anti-war movement grew out of the stimulus provided by the civil rights movement. From 1954 through 1964—that is, from the Supreme Court desegregation decision to the Mississippi voter registration drive —blacks and whites acted together primarily through SDS, SNCC, and CORE. And many civil rights organizations, like SNCC, participated in the anti-war movement, at least at the leadership level. In the 1967 spring mobilization, Stokely Carmichael's contingent of black people marching to the United Nations from Harlem was the rallying point and the highlight of the anti-war protest movement of the day.

The reasons for this sequence of developments are complex. Generally, the claims of blacks to full citizenship rights are understandable to Americans on pragmatic and moral grounds, even if these remain unfulfilled. Furthermore, their "cause" traditionally has been espoused by every left radical group. Strategies and tactics vis-à-vis this cause have sometimes united and sometimes splintered the Left. Nevertheless, it has remained the least controversial issue the Left has put forth insofar as the general public response is concerned. Thus, black protest can generate a momentum to which other issues may become attached—filling out the chorus of radical voices.

By contrast, anti-war movements may appear tainted by

unrealistic idealism or even unpatriotic treachery. American masses are not likely to sympathize with such movements standing independently of morally acceptable ones. The aspirations of blacks follow the traditional struggle for equality by minority and ethnic groupings: there were the struggles of the labor movement for recognition by the larger society, and there were working-class struggles for more popular educational and cultural opportunity. Moreover, all of these were legitimized by some formula familiar to and drawn from American liberalism. However bitter working-class conservatives may be toward extending voting franchise and property rights to include yet another outsider group, their own formula for Americanism leaves them hard-pressed to deny equal treatment (even if separate) to the black people.

The anti-war movement has been predominantly middle-class in background, and remains so to this day. This may help to explain working-class and lower-class opposition to the movement. Stevedores, shopkeepers, sales clerks, mechanics, factory laborers have always been ambivalent and suspicious of causes espoused by the middle-class. Education is viewed paradoxically, both as effete and yet as a model for imitation. Given the educated middle-class character of the anti-war movement, it represents to many working-class Americans a defection from within. War always elicits feelings of patriotism. The demand for rallying behind the nation, without regard for the actual merits of its position, is precisely how "loyalty" comes to be defined. Loyalty is valued more highly than rationality and discussion. Thus, the facts about any war come to be subsumed under the emotions appropriate to all wars.

By contrast, the American black has been traditionally presented as a dilemma and a challenge. Thus it is easier for most of these same working-class Americans to appreciate aggression provoked by the history of racial discrimination and impoverished economic conditions. Furthermore, the black subculture shares many ideals with "grass roots" American culture. The readiness to live with and face violence and death are central virtues for both. It is no accident that the dominant American culture and black militants thus come to share and express resentment for gun control legislation or any curb on the right to bear arms (See Marx, 1967: 170-177).

The anti-war movement, quite to the contrary, has for the most part been in the forefront of efforts to initiate gun-control legislation, and to expand such legislation to institute arms control at police and military levels. We are not here concerned with the purposes to which violent means are employed by one or another social group, only with the fact that the anti-war movement has challenged the basis for resolving problems in American society. Thus, whatever alliance exists between black militants and white anti-war groups is an uneasy one, due not simply to the different composition of each sector of the New Left, but to the different conceptions of strategies and tactics used to achieve their respective ends.

A theme behind most white movements is the idea of self-leadership. They all seek "freedom"; and the freedom sought is the expression and creation of individuality. It is freedom from organization, collectivities, and ultimately rules as such. The black movements seek freedom from white control, not from the constraints of black society. The blacks are trying to create, rather than dissolve, organizational constraints. They do not seek freedom to "do your own thing," but to do the black thing, to find their own identities in subjecting themselves to the discipline of their own collectivities. This is the meaning of dressing, eating, and thinking black, to stand side-by-side with their "soul brothers." In part, the different styles of black and white protest, the tendency to fractionalization among the whites, and to solidarity and discipline among the blacks, are due precisely to contrasting views on organization, no less than to the contents and programs of the respective movements. The white movements draw extreme ideological inferences from the liberal ethic, putting the autonomy of the individual above all organizational constraints. It is the extreme secularized form of Luther's "every man his own priest." The black movements tend to be anti-liberal, dogmatic, sectarian in their direction, affirming the value and supremacy of the collectivity above the individual. In short, for the white movement, the "struggle is the message," but for the black movement the struggle is the necessary price of success.

The black liberation movement makes explicit demands upon the socio-political order. The question of violence and non-violence is largely tactical—the Southern Christian Leadership Conference notwithstanding. The anti-war movement, or at least a dominant wing, retains the belief that its goal is the limitation and ultimately the liquidation of violence. This schism between violence as a tactic (blacks) and violence as an evil (anti-war advocates) separates the two groups, and helps to reveal existing differences between black protest and anti-war protest movements. It is clear that militant blacks are largely disinterested in the course of the war in Vietnam. Indeed, some participants in the black movement seem to think that the war actually may benefit blacks in terms of occupational status. It is not an accident that a basic pitch made by anti-war advocates is that the costs of the war deprive blacks of equality. In fact, little evidence exists that any real correlation of the two phenomena exists. For example, were the war in Vietnam to cease immediately, the overall size of military expenditures for a variety of reasons (rational and irrational) would remain constant over the next five years at least (Weidenbaum, 1967: 60-75; and Little, 1965: 7-9). On the other hand, the structure of the anti-war movement is clearly affected by the comparative lack of black participation. Yet it must continue on its collision course with the military, even if this leads to a confrontation with that large portion of the black community that casts its lot with the Establishment. Certainly one of the fascinating aspects of the future of the anti-war movement is precisely what postures it adopts towards black protest movements that have an avowedly and explicitly violent character. The emergence of organizations such as the Black Panthers in San Francisco-Oakland, the Blackstone Rangers in Chicago, and the Zulu Twelve Hundreds in St. Louis, to name but a few, places a great strain on the anti-war movement—not only philosophically, in terms of goals sought, but practically, in terms of tactics employed.

At the Columbia University disorders in the spring of 1968, and again, at the anti-war demonstrations in Chicago in the summer of 1968, the increasing gap between student movements and black movements became apparent. Black demands were made largely for increased participation, while the anti-war movement increasingly acted in terms of its alienation.

Given the unique role of the student movement in the current anti-war effort, some detailed analysis of this social stratum is in order—not only to show why students become participants, but as an indication of the ferocity of police reaction, and black indifference. For the most part, the backgrounds of participating and sympathetic students in the anti-war movement are not strikingly unusual. There are three broadly discernible groups in the student wing of the anti-war movement.

One: Students from families with middle-class, social service-minded backgrounds. Whether manifesting a high degree of "Christian compassion" or being college-educated social workers, a private and/or political morality concerned with help for the less fortunate was marked. These students often carry the liberal implications of their home experience to greater lengths than parents would have encouraged—but they are not faced with active parental opposition. Many report early experiences of contact with the poor, or, idealizing even to the point of romantic daydreams, a Jew, a black, or someone considered "outside" community, parental, or general social approval.

Two: Students from small-town or suburban communities and strictly conventional homes. These students are faced with a range of parental behavior from physical punishment for political activities to consistent pressure to end political affiliation. These students do not clearly recall early contact with the poor but always sympathized with the "underdog." They are largely inflamed by parental authority and conventionality. Humanizing contact with poverty usually occurred after joining the movement.

Three: Students with parents who were, or are, Communists, Trotskyists—some variety of traditional radical. These are a small, vocal minority within the movement. The parents of these students encourage participation. They are well-versed in Marxist literature, able to take the lead in discussions and other activity. There was frequent contact with small circles of radical friends of parents throughout childhood. The participation of these students has often led to "focus treatments" on the part of right-wing publications.*

Research reveals a number of things about students who participate in peace marches and peace activities:

* In addition to exposés from the Right, a god-that-failed disenchantment, which is a by-product of committed Marxist participants, is now receiving an airing. See ex-Progressive Laborite Philip A. Luce (1966). Through them the movement is "exposed" (as for example a treatment received in the publication of the YAF, *The New Guard* [1965], under the heading "Red Diaper Babies").

(a) Demonstrators, in contrast to leaders, were quite young—the median age being 18-19.

(b) They had no well-formed, comprehensive political ideology.

(c) Many students (though not usually leaders) morally opposed the Cold War and nuclear weapons—in spite of little or no personal religious commitment. Their statements and actions seemed to be idealistic protests for purity.

(d) The age period in which first feelings for social or political "causes" are most likely to develop, data suggest, is 12 to 15.

(e) The majority of students came from politically liberal families, but they were "rebelling" in going far beyond parental experience in the realm of public action. About one-fourth of the students characterized their homes as politically conservative or reactionary. Some demonstrators appeared to display a quality of simultaneous rebellion against identification with parental images.

(f) Older demonstrators, in their middle twenties, seemed to form a separate psycho-social population from the younger students.

(g) Opposing pickets from conservative student groups differed markedly from the peace demonstrators on many parameters of belief and behavior. Comparing the two groups along the psycho-social dimension of trust and distrust is especially interesting (cf. Solomon and Fishman, 1964: 55; and Flacks, 1967: 52-75).

The similarity of backgrounds reveals the distinctiveness of the students' *social* movement. Though each student may have had unique experiences leading him to anti-war participation, his involvement is better explained politically. The strong reaction against conditions and policies in the United States, catalyzed by demands for black rights, has made organization possible and optimism plausible. It is a time that calls forth the "political moralist." As Keniston (1968a: 247-56) indicated in his study of the Vietnam Summer Project of 1967, "although in behavior most of these young radicals were rather *less* violent than their contemporaries, this was not because they were indifferent to the issue, but because their early experience and family values had taught them how to control, modulate, oppose, and avoid violence."

A better appreciation of what is involved in the anti-war movement as a social whole comes from matching ongoing ideologies with social class support. In the first place, there are two broad classifications of anti-war ideologies. The first universal might be called "pacifist," the other "political." Pacifist types tend to be selective in their opposition to modern war.

The most conspicuous type of pacifist is the absolute pacifist, morally committed against bodily harm to others or to himself. This type is usually a religionist or, more specifically, someone who has found little comfort in the organized religions and yet maintains strong theological preferences. As were Tolstoy and Gandhi, these are often men of letters and learning who cluster in marginal religious groups, such as the Fellowship of Reconciliation or Ethical Culture Society, to support premises of absolute pacifism. Such men are in the established sects, professions and occupations.

The second major type consists of religious pacifists per se, those who offer a literal interpretation of the commandment against killing. This group, aside from the political substratum itself, receives support from many of the less educated or at least those less linked with intellectual pursuits who nonetheless deplore violence because of their early church training. Here, traditionalism rather than marginality seems to be the key.

The third kind of pacifist might be called the "thermonuclear pacifist." Here tactical considerations outweigh all other factors. Students in particular espouse, not so much the virtue of life, but the terrors of ultimate weapons. In a sense, thermonuclear pacifists juxtapose conventional war with nuclear annihilation. Recent literature of the culture heroes of the New Left indicates that technological features of modern warfare rather than prohibitions on conflict are central to this group. And the thermonuclear pacifists are by far the largest cluster of people who employ the rubric of pacifism.

As for the political types, they too can be divided into logical (and historical) groups.

First, there are the isolationists, people who are strongly nationalist and who employ the ideology if not the rhetoric of keeping Americans from dying in overseas warfare. The halcyon days of the isolationist movement took place prior to World War II. The America First movement linked up nicely the rhetoric of extreme nationalism with the claims of European fascism—that a policy of non-intervention was best suited to American foreign policy goals.

The ecological settings in which the isolationist wing of the anti-war movement had its greatest strength—Chicago, St. Louis, Dallas—indicate that the agrarian sector, or at least the midwest organized working class, was greatly committed to this framework. This kind of ideology is still prevalent, judging by the information available in the editorial columns of midwest newspapers in such middle-sized cities as Topeka, Omaha, or Joplin. The transformation of the agrarian middle class into a *nouveau riche* urban middle class had tended to wipe out this isolationist wing of the anti-war movement, not to mention the fact that fascism as a world historic force was destroyed as the result of World War II. Yet this type of position remains in evidence not so much in the anti-war movement as currently constituted as in the unorthodox sentiments expressed in the major parties and reflected in the national polls on the war.

The second political type might be called the "federalist." He believes in one world, in a "United States of the World." He sees the "war system" as a product of competing nation-states; the solution, therefore, is a unified political world system. But the federalists too are found at the margins of orthodox politics. When the equilibrium between the underdeveloped world and the fully industrialized world dissolved into open and intense rivalry after World War II and when the major powers retained their strong nationalist sentiments in the structuring of the United Nations, the federalists lost favor. The formation of a United Nations Organization which maintains rather than dissolves national sovereignties has effectively liquidated federalism as a political force, and eroded its base in any social sector of the population.

The third political type to be found in the anti-war movement, and by far the most numerous, is issue-oriented. He is specifically concerned with ending the war in Vietnam, be it on the basis of economic issues—for one, that the war on poverty is frustrated by the war overseas—or on personal ones, with the Vietnam War seen as a direct threat to students' careers via the military draft, as well as to his own vision of what the good society should be.

There is an obvious overlap between the thermonuclear pacifists and the issue-oriented political types. Both groups draw their greatest sustenance from the 8 million student population, the 20 million black population, and the more than 6 million persons of Mexican and Puerto Rican backgrounds. And this huge "underclass" can command the support of at least a healthy minority of the "intellectual class."

A fourth political type is anti-war only in a limited sense: he is opposed to the Vietnam War *because* America intervened against the revolutionary side. He advocates revolution as the only way to create needed social, political, and economic changes in the Third World. He supports wars that aid the revolutionary cause, and opposes wars that injure such causes. This type defines himself as anti-imperialist and believes that the Unites States' economic, political, and military presence must be expelled from the Third World, by revolutionary military means if necessary. For this group, the successful Cuban Revolution serves as a model.

The anti-imperialists seek an NLF victory rather than simply an end to the war in Vietnam. They oppose actions which would end the war on terms that they consider unacceptable, just as North Vietnam in the Paris Peace Talks indicates an unwillingness to negotiate an end to the war on unfavorable terms. This group is not anti-war since it accepts war as a legitimate and valid military strategy.

This group seeks an end to imperialism rather than an end to war. It is opposed to the negotiated settlement of the war on any terms except the total and unconditional withdrawal of American troops. It is opposed to gun-control legislation in America, on the grounds that such legislation would deprive the revolutionary movement in this country of access to weapons. Finally, it is beginning to talk about revolutionary confrontation with the American military—in the form of police and National Guard. In this respect, it sees the role of police in America as similar to the role of the American military in Vietnam and many other nations. Both are a force that must be defeated for a successful revolution to occur. There exists within the American anti-war movement an element, numerically small but increasingly influential (or at least vocal), that is anti-American rather than anti-administration.

The correlation between all these types and their social bases of support would require extensive empirical analysis.* For our purposes it is sufficient to point out that participation of marginal political types and deviant social subcultures indicates the drawing power of the anti-war issue as a vehicle for expressing a fundamental sense of alienation. For one thing is clear: any minimization or elimination of thermonuclear pacifists and issue-oriented "peaceniks" would quickly reduce the size of the anti-war movement to the sect-like proportions it had in more tranquil times.

The continuation of the Vietnam War provides common ground for the diverse organizational and ideological facets of

---

* Some studies indicate that key leadership of the student wing of the anti-war movement had parents who were themselves radicals. This supports the thesis of generational continuity no less than generational revolt.

the anti-war movement. And as the war escalates and endures, the claims of the "anti-imperialists" tend to be substantiated in the eyes of the "issue-oriented" participants. It also inhibits major differences between the various factions from surfacing. Though not fatally flawed by the factionalism of the past, the peace movement is fractionated and atomistic. Some 150 organizations are classified as anti-Vietnam protest groups; 75 to 100 are specifically anti-draft. Any organizational chart grossly misrepresents the fluidity and disorganization of the groups; however, it does give some sense of the movement's scope.

The National Mobilization Committee to End the War in Vietnam, known in some quarters as MOB or "the Mob," tops the pyramid by reaching down to contact leading national and community coalition groups. In New York, the Fifth Avenue Peace Parade Committee to End the War in Vietnam, once headed by Mobilization director David Dellinger, performs the basic organizational work needed for mass rally. Most large cities have similar coalitions.

Responsible for activating the long list of national and local groups in its area, the Fifth Avenue Peace Parade Committee will contact a number of adult peace, and primarily pacifist, groups: Women Strike for Peace, SANE, War Resisters' League, Committee for Nonviolent Action, and the Fellowship of Reconciliation. For student support, SDS, Student Peace Union, and the Student Mobilization Committee are primary. There are three groups for veterans— Veterans for Peace, Vietnam Veterans to End the War in Vietnam, and Veterans and Reservists to End the War in Vietnam, of which the last is the most militant. That is, they are more willing to use direct action, risk arrest, and turn in their military medals and papers. Anti-draft organizations include the Resistance (supporters of draft card burnings, draft refusers, and allied seminary students who refuse religious deferment and insist on conscientious-objector status) and black anti-draft groups. Most professions, from writing to academics, have numerous ad hoc organizations aimed at war protest just as the clergy and religious organizations do. These include the Episcopal Peace Fellowship, Concerned Clergy, Catholic Peace Fellowship and American Friends Service Committee. Since the Spring Mobilization in 1967, Reform Democratic Clubs have participated in the New York movement, helping in turn to transform the war issue into a respectable political one. Other political organizations contacted for mass mobilizations are the left-wing, multi-issue groups like the Communist Party and the Socialist Workers Party. Some unions, such as the ILGWU, Local 1199 of the Amalgamated Workers Union and District 635, are also counted on for support. Currently, the emphasis in New York is on geographical organizing on a block by block level. Charles Street and West 84th Street have groups whose major goal is peace in Vietnam.

Including the local, citywide, regional, and national committees, by 1968 there were in all some 150 groups. Some perform distinctive roles. Women Strike for Peace, for example, is as much a fund-raising as it is a direct-action group. Membership lists, of course, overlap as people may ally themselves with church, professional, and single-issue organizations.

The characters and relations of these diverse organizations are fluid. Despite its overwhelming publicity and tactical advantage, most people in the coalition organizations claim that SDS has not been influential in the mobilizations. "They usually come in at the end," as they did at the Pentagon. Once dominant in the early peace movement, the Committee for Nonviolent Action, founded by the late A. J. Muste, is now at best a regional grouping in the Northeast. Committed to nonviolent action as a total philosophy of life, it is most similar to the Gandhian spirit of civil disobedience.

Youth Against War and Fascism consider themselves to be

radical. In New York, they marched without a permit, as did the Committee to Aid the Liberation Front and the Veterans and Reservists. Most noteworthy is the increasing militancy of the clergy from support to halting the bombing in 1965 to the October 1967 Call to Resist Illegitimate Authority. At that time 320 clergymen pledged that they would aid and abet draft refusers and transform synagogues and churches into sanctuaries for conscientious objectors. Also important is the formation in September 1967 of Business Executives Move for Vietnam Peace. Most are managers or owners of middle-sized businesses.

The mobilizing role of the intellectuals can scarcely be underestimated. They challenged the basic assumptions of the war, and they examined the inconsistencies and in-accuracies made by government officials. Beyond that, they dramatized the generalized destructiveness associated with the strategy of the war of attrition. In other words, they offered the counterlegitimacy of Science over and against the legitimacy of Government. And for that reason, their author-ity far exceeded their numbers.

In a sense, the very unity of the intellectuals depended upon the binding force of the war issue. Through criticism of the Vietnam conflict, journalists could challenge the premises of the day-to-day conduct of the war; logicians and philoso-phers could challenge the inconsistencies of the war rationale; scientists could decry the growing uses of bacteriological and chemical weaponry; and literati could once more take up the classic claims of humanism and civilization.

In fact, the intellectuals were more important in mobiliz-ing sentiment than even past clusters of men of ideas were in respect to revolutionary parties. The reason is precisely that classical political leadership does not exist in the anti-war movement. And in such a context, only the force of ideas, the men of ideas, comes to gain universal attention. The heroic proportion of poets like Robert Lowell, philosophers like Herbert Marcuse, journalists like Bernard Fall, and novelists like Mary McCarthy and Norman Mailer looms larger precisely because standard political types are held in disrepute.

Anti-politics, or better, the politics of moralism, characterizes the anti-war protest movement, as it has traditionally characterized intellectual postures toward political leadership. This frame of mind was well summed up by the freelance photographer at the Pentagon March who observed: "There was no leadership, that was what was so beautiful. The leaders all think they're leaders, but this just happened." And not waiting for the Fifth Avenue Peace Parade Committee to put out a call to picket Hubert Humphrey's opening campaign at the Labor Day Parade, large numbers of individuals turned out to protest his stand on the war and on the Chicago demonstrations.

To say that the movement is "organized" would give exaggerated credit to the leadership and the methods used for mobilizing mass demonstrations. Loose confederations or temporary coalitions today exist as pragmatic necessities in the new world of leftist politics. Students, upon whom the movement is largely based and through whom it has become legitimate, disdain the old-time popular front and its factionalism. Despite the peace movement, the styles of the young—in rhetoric, dress, and language—have changed. For them, existential action plus the rhetoric of contemporary revolution is a style as well as an ideology. Small groups, organized for specific ends, become the ideal. The ones that carry with them some mystical aura, some communism of the mind as it were, become those that the students take particular pleasure in identifying with.

The newer style anti-war leader is basically a model, and not a chief. He does not function as a classic charismatic, much less bureaucratic, head. Many leaders are heroes of the movement's past crusades, serving as models for the followers who can then pattern their behavior and action in the same way, although they would not be available to "take orders" from the leaders if the latter tried to give them. This is a new political reality. Because of the ease of communication among "mass intellectuals" in American society, it is relatively simple to start a nationwide movement based on emulation. However, "responsible authorities" can only seem to appreciate such phenomena by thinking of organization—secret or manifest. The point is that a high degree of organization is not necessary if communication of ideas and sentiments is rapid and extensive enough to persuade some segment of the public to become involved in mass activities.

The Youth International Party, or Yippies, particularly demonstrate the theatrical, half-for-real sensibility that appeals to the students' sense of humor and sense of outrage at the war. Despite their reputation (one estimate placed their number at ten), their only outstanding accomplishment is their finely developed sense of public relations. One could say that they attack the mimeograph machine more than the on-duty patrolman. But the Yippie myth prevails and grows stronger as more people—even those who are unsympathetic—believe what they say.

For the young, then, such older, left-wing political groups as the Communist Party and the Trotskyite Socialist Workers Party are "out of it." Ironically, official response to the demonstrators is directed toward these outsiders. During the early days of the movement, it was common to hear political leaders call the demonstrators Communists or victims of Communist exploitation.

Students have become increasingly militant and intransigent as the war has progressed. The peace movement has filtered down into the high schools. In some measure, the peace issue seems to highlight fears of the military draft and also discontent with school programming and administrations. The campuses are now the pacesetters for the peace movement. The formation in 1968 of the Student Mobilization Committee to End the War in Vietnam formally indicated the passing of power to the young. What was once disregarded by the adult peace movement has become its central strategy. The SDS policy of grass roots, community organization over mass mobilization was recently adopted by the National Mobilization Committee.

Propaganda of the word, characteristic of the genteel tradition from which the anti-war movement emerges, has been replaced by propaganda of the deed, a characteristic of the younger and more recent entries into protest and confrontational politics. In this sense there has been a startling change from alienation to commitment and now to revolution-making.

The peace movement of the past deeply linked most *traditional* organizations involved to various American elites. Peace groups, from the Carnegie Endowment for International Peace to the United Nations support agencies, have maintained long and strong ties to Congress. Organizations such as SANE are committed to maintaining ties with the Establishment and with the various elements within the governmental structure of power. The newer organizations often ignore tie-ins with established power. In fact, they repudiate precisely these connections as futile and even faulty in conception. Thus, the gulf is not simply between newer violent types of response and older non-violent types of organizations. Often the correlation can be made between the *newer violent* organizations and the appeals to mass action, and the *older non-violent* organizations and appeals to elite decision-making.

The anti-war movement has evolved into a frontal assault on traditional American notions of patriotism. The symbolic defiance of common American values has reached a point where burning of the American flag or the raising of the Viet Cong flag is now something of a ritual. The New York demonstrations in April 1967 used the California demonstrations as a model. Nearly all of the confrontations between demonstrators and counter-demonstrators took place over control of the Viet Cong flag. In point of fact, however, the peace movement itself was torn over the question of symbolic assault on American patriotism versus discussion with the power system over the "real issues." Organizations such as SANE and the American Friends Service Committee were particularly divided over the new tactics. Only with great difficulty did the movement as a whole reconcile itself to wholesale assaults on the American value system. The switch is hard for the traditionalists of protest, who are sentimental about traditional American symbols. The new protesters, however, burn the flags but still consider themselves the true embodiment of these symbols.

Symbolism had always been a consistent element of the anti-war protest, from the place of action—the Pentagon and Independence Hall—to its timing—Thanksgiving Day, July 4th, the anniversaries of Hiroshima and Nagasaki. The most symbolic acts, burning draft cards and carrying the Viet Cong flag, have generated the most violence. They assault the romantic, irrational, and powerful identification of man with country.

This, too, illustrates that violence is often a consequence of behavior. It is not the purpose of anti-war rallies to become military battlefields. The natural history of the crowd situation itself breeds violence. Conflict occurs mostly in unstructured situations where mass congregations of people with different points of view coalesce into opposing (but reinforced) factions. They become enmeshed in a zero-sum situation where one side or the other is compelled to retreat or surrender.

The definite shift from the politics of symbolic opposition to the actual prevention of war activities that support and sustain the war is another mark of the movement today. The direct action, of course, tends to raise the ante and to increase the level of violence. Confrontations may be prolonged and involve such fundamental questions as the control of property, the authority of university officials, and even the ownership of buildings, streets and empty lots. The amount of violence seems to be directly related to the intimacy of the participants with the institution under attack. Confrontation sought and made with such sensitive federal military functions as ROTC training programs yields the most violence. Though this may mark a turn to guerrilla insurgency, it more obviously reflects an escalation in the symbolic struggle.

The terms of dialogue in American life have been directly affected by the anti-war movement. The increasing frustration over the conduct of the Vietnam War has polarized a population reared on a diet of victory and defeat and unable to accept a permanent state of war. As the Vietnam War has continued, it has also become the subject of popular debate. The question of American overseas commitment has been picked up by orthodox political actors, and not just theatrical leftists.

When the government mobilizes support and force, opposition groups work extra hard to weaken the government stand. Thus, as the government and the broad population debate the war issue, and infuse it into the political process, violent defiance of the law and left-wing counterforce generally decrease. Violence in relation to the law can more readily be diminished, not by the suppression of discussion, but rather by its promulgation. For in a very real sense the legitimation of democracy entails the conversion of the anti-war movement into a specialized group.

In that sense, the radical wing of the anti-war protest

movement—thermonuclear pacifists and issue-oriented politicos alike—is subject to what might be called the iron law of defeat through victory. The broadening involvement of mass numbers into intensive discussion on the nature of the war tends to subvert violent response. Thus, the Presidential campaign of Eugene McCarthy was, in the main, disparaged by the SDS leadership, who did not participate in the primary campaign struggles. The McCarthy organization and the SDS were antagonists, vying for the same constituency.

The anti-war movement, through the very intensification of its polemics and the very magnitude of its organization (even apart from the orthodox party system) is a potential source for reducing rather than stimulating violence. This is the intent, if not always the result, of peace. For what one commentator has recently noted about the young is equally true for the anti-war movement as a whole.

> The primary task is to develop new psychological, political, and international controls on violence. Indeed, many of the dilemmas of today's young radicals seem related to their extraordinarily zealous efforts to avoid any action or relationship in which inner or outer violence might be evoked. Distaste for violence animates the profound revulsion many of today's youth feel toward the war in Southeast Asia, just as it underlies a similar revulsion against the exploitation or control of man by man. . . . Even the search for forms of mass political action that avoid physical violence—a preference severely tested and somewhat undermined by the events of recent months—points to a considerable distaste for the direct expression of aggression (Keniston, 1968b: 243).

The involvement of masses in the political process, by affecting major decisions, reduces the possibility of violence so long as there is a reasonable chance that the normal political process might yield an end to the war.

In these terms, the future behavior of young politically-minded people is central. If they feel that the political system cheated them out of a legitimate victory, that it is not representative of the American people, and that it can only be sustained in its present form by police tactics, then the chances for escalated violence are high. If, on the other hand, they accept the legitimacy of their defeat, and feel that they had a chance to present their case to the American people and the people decided against their position, then mass mobilization will have helped reduce the potential for violence.

Since leaders in both major parties have adopted roughly similar positions, the Vietnam War will probably not be a viable issue in party politics, despite its centrality as the major concern of American public opinion. Thus, the chances of mass participation by the anti-war movement in the legitimate political process are slight. A political program which directly confronts the inability of the political party system to offer a real alternative on the war has now been developed by the radical arm of the anti-war movement. This even includes plans for disruption of the election mechanism. It is impossible to determine yet whether this will materialize, but if it does, high levels of violence on both sides can be predicted. But violence is often neither the goal nor the essential tactic of the movement. Too often it is the byproduct of the conduct of political struggle by other means.

Violence is such a tough-sounding and ultimate word that it is easy to overlook the simplest point of all: violence is often a surrogate for revolution. As Barrington Moore (1968: 11) so aptly noted: "It is untrue that violence settles nothing. It would be closer to the mark to assert that violence has settled all historical issues so far, and most of them in the wrong way." The revolutionary process begins with seemingly spontaneous violence on the part of formerly inchoate groups in society. Translating violence into the anti-war movement requires two parallel phenomena: There must be a felt need on the part of large, unsponsored groups to participate in the decision-making process, and, at the same time, there must also be enough closure in the political order to prevent the absorption of such groups into the customary structure of decision-making. We can hardly do better than conclude this chapter with a remarkable quote by Staughton Lynd (1968b: 172) on the alienated nature of protest politics in the United States:

> All that had been closed and mysterious in the procedure of the parent institution becomes open and visible in the workings of its counterpart. Decision-makers, appointed to the former, are elected to the latter. Parallel bodies in different places begin to communicate, to devise means of coordination: a new structure of representation develops out of direct democracy and is controlled by it. Suddenly, in whole parts of the country and in entire areas of daily life, it becomes apparent that people are obeying the new organs of authority rather than the old ones. Finally, an act or a series of acts of legitimation occur. . . . The task becomes building into the new society something of that sense of shared purpose and tangibly shaping a common destiny which characterized the revolution at its most intense.

One difficulty is that this new source of legitimation remains highly restricted to a small segment of society. As Kenneth Boulding (1965: 18-20) indicates, when a nation provides even a minimum rhetorical respect to a value, such as racial integration, protest movements can afford to be disruptive. But without widespread commitment to a value, such as pacifism, successful protest movements must be calm, educational, and basically respectable. Otherwise the protest itself becomes the object of controversy, which creates a strong backlash. Thus, whether protest brings a new legitimation or a new backlash depends, in part at least, on the values of the public.

RESPONSES

5 BY AUTHORITIES

TO THE ANTI-WAR MOVEMENT

Extremely important are the assumptions underlying the behavior of both police and demonstrators. For police, the defense of law and order is the primary concern. They envision themselves maintaining the statutory law against informal norms of behavior. Police tend to view anti-war demonstrators as disrupters, malcontents who use exaggerated tactics to promote nihilism and anarchism. The demonstrators view the police as brutes who use exaggerated responses—"overkill"—precisely to the degree that they lack moral authority for their actions. Thus, both demonstrators and police suffer from problems of maintaining legitimacy.

The task of determining the causal sequence of events in mass riots has plagued analysts of spontaneous or mass behavior since the beginning of the century. The main question is clear: Why does protest sometimes move to the street? The answer clearly inheres in the ability of any given policy to absorb rather than alienate new groups striving for power and legitimation.

The role of the police is central in the control of the anti-war movement, since it is the local police force that has primary, or at least immediate, responsibility. Several important points must therefore be made. First, the size of the police force has remained relatively constant over the past quarter century. In 1940 full-time police employees numbered 1.7 percent of the population. By 1966 this figure rose only slightly, to 2.0 percent. Second, what has changed is the amount of money spent on police at all governmental levels—particularly the Department of Defense. Here we find a per capita expenditure in 1940 of 2.92 percent of the total federal budget, while by 1966 this figure leaps to 15.91 percent. This leads to our third point. If the size of the police force is relatively constant and we presume that general living rates increase evenly in a scale of wage distribution, then the huge increase in the portions spent on police must be for technological innovation. So police "hardware" has indeed become a key issue.

If the measure was simply that of physical prowess, an administration would require roughly one police officer for every two guerrilla insurgents to maintain order. But this ratio changes dramatically once "non-lethal" weapons are introduced, for technology greatly increases the odds of the police. Once the matter is reduced to a discussion of "hardware," the anti-war forces are almost compelled to switch their tactics to guerrilla insurgency. The use of tear gas or Mace by police is a contingency the anti-war protestors must prepare for. They do, with protective devices, or even offensive devices to prevent the use of these weapons. The police, in turn, interpret this readiness to employ counterforce as proof of violent intent, and the whole shooting match begins again. Thus, the very insistence of the police and their supporters on having exclusive use of weapons of limited potency tends to sharpen debate and reduce still further the area of political legitimacy.

Demonstrations do not occur in a vacuum. In any given confrontation, both the anti-war movement and police bring with them a set of past experiences and expectations that influence their behavior. Thus, the local history of confrontation between political radicals and police greatly influences the level of violence in the anti-war movement. For example, the level of violence is greatest on the West Coast, particularly in the Bay Area—Berkeley-Oakland-San Francisco. This is understandable in terms of its local history. The Berkeley HUAC demonstrations, which were approximately at the level of violence typical of the present stage of student rebellion and anti-war movements elsewhere, occurred even earlier than the main thrust of the civil rights movement. While its national impact was minimal, its local impact, in terms of shaping the future of political confrontations, was important.

The HUAC demonstrations were followed by a second major student confrontation with the police—the Free Speech Movement at Berkeley. Again, hundreds of students were forcibly removed from a building and arrested. While there were some charges of police misconduct, there was no reported violence on either side. In fact, there never have been "riots" on the Berkeley campus, media exaggerations notwithstanding. From the perspective of the police, the third major event was the emergence of a highly organized and militant black liberation movement: the San Francisco-Oakland area is the home of the Black Panthers. Conflict with the Panthers marked a major escalation in political violence for the police.

At the same time, the anti-war movement in the Bay Area was more militant than the movement anyplace else in the country. It stopped troop trains in Oakland and sabotaged ROTC programs at Berkeley and Stanford. To some extent, this reflects geography: Oakland is a major depot for soldiers being sent to Vietnam, and thus a major target which does not exist elsewhere. But their militancy also reflects the history of the student movement and of labor radicalism in the area. It covers a long time span in which many less militant tactics had failed. But even in the Berkeley area, the anti-war "assault" is on state property rather than private persons. It was obstructive rather than physically aggressive.

There is thus an accumulation of hostility and frustration on both sides. In any event, it is not possible to describe the dynamics of violence in the present anti-war movement without taking into account the accumulated heritage of both sides. Chicago is another example of the influence of local history on the nature of conflict. For whatever reasons, Chicago has long been a center of radical political organizing. It is the national office of the Students for a Democratic Society; it is the first northern city in which a major attempt at civil rights organizing was made; and it is the first city in which a serious attempt at working-class and middle-class white organizing has been made. At the same time, it is a last bastion of the "boss"-run local party machine. Thus, so much control is centered in the mayor's hands that the city's political style and capacity to handle problems arising from a shifting national scene is not susceptible to corrective advice or example from "outside."

For that reason, Mayor Daley could afford to allow, and even order, the Chicago Police Department to use massive force to put down anti-war demonstrations, both before and after the Democratic Party Convention. The local autonomy of Chicago, and the relative immunity of the Chicago Police Department from outside influences, are major factors in the nature of the demonstrations which occurred during the Convention.

Chicago and Oakland both have local histories of harassment of the anti-war movement which favored stepped-up violence. Not only was there harassment of public meetings, but also of private parties and private persons on trumped-up charges. Related to this is the two-year history of friction with the militant civil rights groups, particularly the Blackstone Rangers in Chicago and the Black Panthers in Oakland.

Since there was no effective sanctioning or reprimanding of the police in the past, they clearly had no expectation of undue trouble from their handling of the peace demonstrators.

Local causes, however, have not prevented police behavior from having national effects. Among other things, local police actions have provided the national anti-war movement with models of police brutality and with justifications for stepping up anti-police tactics among demonstrators. Thus, local police provide the radical movement nationally with a visible "enemy." Easily identifiable generally by uniform, and by regular responses to demonstrations, the police have become a surrogate for the frustrations of the New Left.

It is not that the various analyses made of police are incorrect, or even imprudent; rather, the implications drawn from the facts are either not made or made inaccurately. (1) The police do indeed come from the lower middle-class sectors, strongholds of "working-class authoritarianism." (2) They do "overreact" to anti-war demonstrators (among others). (3) They do think and act like soldiers fighting guerrilla insurgency. (4) And finally, their hierarchical organization encourages anti-democratic values and behavior. However, these do not add up to a meaningful analysis.

In the first place, the lower middle class does not make the decisions in American political life. They tend to be overshadowed and outmaneuvered by the ethnic minorities and student population from "below," and the traditional bastions of power from "above." Second, while the police "overreacted" to the protests surrounding the Democratic National Convention in Chicago, it was just as much a response to attacks on the Chicago Police Department (and Superintendent Conlisk) for being "soft on black looters" of West Side Chicago in the riots that occurred in April 1968. Third, while police learned tactics attuned to the problems of "internal war," they were under extremely powerful constraints ranging from the community knowledge of police officers to their lack of effective numbers to combat guerrillas. Finally, despite their organizational hierarchy, policemen exhibit tremendous variations from top to bottom, and from community to community. Police organization, however militaristic, is fundamentally different from an army: Membership is voluntary rather than compulsory; it is locally rather than nationally organized; it has no clearly defined purpose, such as defining an "enemy."

Cressey and Elgesem (1968: 55,59) have indicated that the police are also more reactors than initiators of political actions. They are charged with implementing conflicting theories of society within a framework of conformity. The police are being "just" when they strictly invoke the law, and contrariwise, when they overlook offenses by using discretion. The whole range of "mitigating circumstances" is the gray area whereby the police establish their own forms of legitimation. Precisely the direct denial of such latitude by the anti-war protesters excites police against demonstrators. For the protesters not only assault the law abstractly, but consciously and defiantly reject the "law enforcement" role upon which the police rest their claims for material and moral service to the community.

Like demonstrators, police also respond to visible symbols. It is likely that they object more to blacks and unwashed hippies and Yippies than to the anti-war movement as such. Police ideology on the issue of war generally, and the Vietnam War in particular, probably reflects nationalistic tendencies. But in the context of a demonstration the police are responding to "law-breakers," to minorities for which they may harbor distaste, to challenges to their own status and prejudices. Often they are reacting to symbolic acts deeply offensive to their lower middle-class values, rather than to the anti-war sentiment. The burning of American flags, the raising of Viet Cong flags, and other such acts are what probably stimulate police violence. Police are hostile to gross actions rather than points of view. And they are moved to violence partly because of their working-class belief that "decent" men must forcefully defend what is important to them. They have worked hard to get where they are and so they are easily inflamed by challenges to their status. Thus "decency" and personal pride demand the art of "manly defense" in the abstract, that is, on principle. The idea that this may lead to or actually constitute "brutality" is difficult for police to understand.

An elusive, yet vital, aspect of police-community relations is that there are, and always have been, groups in society against whom violence has been informally and traditionally sanctioned: homosexuals, bohemians, racial minorities, etc. This is very important, because these groups no longer accept their outcast status as a reasonable basis for discrimination. And now that social "deviants" have been joined by political "marginals," the weight of their claims on society has multiplied. If the police are to cope more satisfactorily with this phenomenon they will have to be made more aware of their own implication in a selective rather than universal approach to law and order. And for this to take place, a combination of mass education and increasing local control will probably be required.

As we move from the police and their mission of defending "law and order" to the legal apparatus and its basis in "justice tempered with mercy," we can also see that "police brutality" may have grown out of police frustrations with what they feel to be the deferential treatment of the "criminals" they bring in. Legal statutes regulating treatment of offenders are deliberately formulated as universals to defend the individual against assault no matter what his beliefs. But the particulars of an arrest derive from specific behavior. Demonstrators can be booked for "disturbing the peace" or "destroying property," but they cannot be punished for the causes they espouse. Hence, the police often feel that demonstrators are getting away with minor charges and penalties for major crimes which damage the "American system."

Ultimately the "authorities," the repositories of national power, have been the legislative and executive branches of government. Here the problems of the anti-war movement are far graver than those of the black rights movement. For support of the black underclass, at least at the level of rhetoric, is far more extensive than any support basis for the anti-war movement. After all, the equality of black citizens in the United States is part of official federal policy, not only before the law but as it is embodied in hundreds of pieces of legislation, thousands of memoranda, and even national commissions sanctioned by presidential authority. However, opposition to the Vietnam War, and to the United States foreign policy generally, has little legislative support and even less executive support. Indeed, whatever legislation does exist—from the Tonkin Gulf Resolution to the executive orders mobilizing portions of the National Guard—tends to shape a national consensus in favor of the conflict. In this sense, there is greater authorization to beat the heads of anti-war demonstrators than of civil rights demonstrators.

Legal support for the anti-war movement has rested on defense of the right to demonstration, rather than on the rights of the issue behind a demonstration. It is this right to demonstrate which policemen have difficulty justifying. For if it leads to violence, or anti-patriotic outrages against the flag, how can it be a popular right? As men, they feel called upon to defend American virtues. They would need to be "philosophers" to defend rights of demonstrators to vigorous anti-government protests. This is too great a demand for a limited police background. Thus, police are left tense and unsatisfied by the minor punishments and legal defenses extended to arrested demonstrators, and may be supplementing "justice" in the context of a demonstration by adding the heavier penalties they feel are deserved by the offender but omitted by the legal process.

The peace movement itself, quite apart from the black rights movement, is increasingly singled out for criticism at the federal level. The "force" of the state responded to the "violence" of the movement by an attempt to isolate its leadership. The strategy backfired. First, the anti-war movement has no refined "leadership" in the same sense as the Communist Party in the late forties had a leading cadre. Second, the legitimacy of a federal court sentencing no longer represents an effective deterrent to direct action. The peace movement took its cue from the Nuremberg Trial conviction of the Nazi leadership, which held that the responsibility for life is a higher obligation than obedience to national law.

Men who have been put on trial often represent organizational forces: for example, Benjamin Spock in relation to SANE, Marcus Raskin in relation to the Institute of Policy Studies, Reverend Tristram Coffin in relation to the Christian Ministerial Movement Against the War. Each of these organizations is a major voice in the war resistance movement. The men chosen and singled out by the government for prosecution were each in their own way part of the informal leadership of the non-Communist Left.

The growth in the range of anti-war protest movements, itself a reaction to the hostility exhibited for quasi-respectable figures, has led to increasing frustrations on the part of the demonstrators and the authorities. Since government response to demonstrations has often been the demand for investigation of the demonstrators, and rarely the reconsideration of the nature of American foreign policy commitments, the escalation of violence by younger peace groups is in some measure a demand to be taken seriously.

In 1965 the Attorney General's office said that the Justice Department would investigate Communist influence in the anti-Vietnam protest movement. This indicated the growing willingness of the federal government to impose heavier penalties. Other indications of implicit threats against the protesters included legislative investigations of the peace movement and executive office statements that even well-meaning demonstrators can become victims of Communist exploitation. The charge that demonstrators are wrong in their assessments of the American presence in Vietnam and therefore unpatriotic runs through the whole government response to the peace movement. The head of the Selective Service System, in fact, ordered the reclassification of leading student protesters as draftable. These military and political forces available to the administration are an important element in the change of anti-war tactics from nonviolence to counterviolence.

The practiced politician, in the inevitable process of specialization, becomes adept at managing and pacifying his constituency. The representative role is inherently conservative, as responsibility for representing varied interests and maintaining professional prestige make it impossible to isolate the "peace issue." It is not the task of congressional representatives to plead the case of one sector, but to represent the whole community. Even the politician who reaches Congress on a peace plank can scarcely afford a singular dedication to one "issue." Idealistic leadership is an art in itself and a luxury which the representative finds difficult to afford, even when he is inclined to consider it. Thus, the idealistic peace activist performs, in a practical way, a task for which no specialized professional leadership exists. Anti-war politics is thus a specialty which marginal groups can afford precisely because they are not constrained by the electoral processes.

The response to state force cannot be fully measured by

the general increase in the propensity to violence in the society or by an increase in the escalation of the war. For the *availability* of instruments of destruction, rather than the desirability of violence as a method, is an important index to the level of mass violence.

The anti-war movement has registered genuine successes. The tactics of confrontation and disruption have, it would seem, been increasingly successful since they were first employed at the University of California in 1964. The model, of course, was the civil rights struggle of the previous decade. It has changed policies on the university level; the University of Chicago and Columbia University no longer give out class rankings to the Selective Service System. Confrontation has also increased the cost of the war: the two-day March on the Pentagon cost the government $1 million, the mobilization of army personnel and National Guardsmen for this event alone accounting for more than half of the cost. The expectation that other tactics of disruption would be at least as successful in terms of making it costly for the government to move against demonstrators may partially be responsible for the increased stakes introduced by the police and National Guard.

Despite the surprisingly few counterdemonstrators at the anti-war rallies, resentment of pacifist life styles (although not necessarily of the anti-war movement as a whole) among the American people continues. At critical occasions this spills over into violent responses to the communism of the mind engaged in by some radical groups. Throughout the United States, they have developed a string of "communal farms" or "community living centers" that have directly affected ordinary citizen property-holders. One farm in Voluntown, Connecticut, was the scene of a gun battle between police and alleged members of the right-wing Minutemen organization. On August 24, 1968, the Minutemen invaded and apparently intended to burn down a farm inhabited by pacifists.

Owned by the Committee for Nonviolent Action, the farm and its old-guard liberal pacifists, draft resisters, and apolitical hippies had enraged not only the extreme Right but the local citizenry as well. One shipfitter who works on submarines commented: "We never get into the news until they come around here. I see them come to the post-office. They're a cruddy bunch. They don't wash up and shave. They're always mailing pamphlets out." A housewife and mother of five echoed the same sentiment in supporting the Minutemen attack: "The only time you see the town in the paper is pacifists this and pacifists that. We wish they'd leave. They're very different. We steer clear. The pacifists seem to breed trouble, like anybody that different and that way out." Allowing that he misdirected visitors to the pacifist community, a part-time policeman stated that although he had never been to the farm, he wished "they'd get the hell out. The beards and the filth they live in . . ." (cf. Shipler, 1968).

The dilemma of the anti-war communalists, and others as well, is that as they attempt to live by the canons of nonviolence, they accentuate and underscore cultural differences that can lead to violence. In such a situation the anti-war protesters, either in private or public demonstrations of faith in the peaceful way, are compelled to call upon police protection for their continued survival. They are thus compelled to live in a world of hostility to the police and of relative dependence on them; while they violate the law in the name of conscience, they must also demand legal protection.

This raises the larger issue of the connection between middle-class peace protest groups and violent working-class groups. Their struggle is not really over philosophical values, or even ideological beliefs, but over cultural norms of standards of sexuality, cleanliness, racial interaction, and general sociability. Here too we can observe the delicate thread which connects the substance of peace movements to the styles of the peace advocates; as we noted before, violence can take place just as readily, if not more so, over considerations of class styles as over substantive issues.

CONFRONTATION

VERSUS 6

REPRESENTATION

The problems introduced by the revamped anti-war movement are novel enough in structure and fluid enough in content to make any set of conclusions extremely tenuous. Yet,
certain implications seem clear for the future of American
society and politics if the current drift turns into a full-scale
tide.

Foremost is the implication that confrontational politics
has become a direct challenge to representational politics.
The past quarter of a century has witnessed the extraordinary
increase of expertise in policy-making and politics. Ap-
pointed experts have increased more rapidly than have duly
elected officials. This has weakened the ordinary citizen's
participation through voting and familiarity with the political
process generally. As a result his apathy toward representative politics increases in the face of challenges. Meanwhile, representative politicians have grown more pressed by
their technical inadequacies and reliance upon the expert
bureaucracy and are increasingly limited by enlarging but

fragmenting interest claims and counterclaims within their constituencies. Their frequently ineffectual actions have undermined their public prestige until they are now being severely tried by confrontational politics. Thoughtless support of the war in Vietnam has further marked them as a target for confrontation as protest has increased on the issue. Thus the United States overseas military involvement has come down to a test of professional representatives.

The arguments of the experts against parliamentarians are familiar. The time span for critical decision-making is now a matter of minutes, not years. Constituencies inhibit and restrain elected officials from exercising proper decisions at decisive moments. Political figures are ill-equipped by a narrow legal training to cope with wide-ranging social problems. But advocates of confrontational politics, with slight modification, make the same charges against representational politics. Bruce L. R. Smith (1968: 111-128) has caught the spirit of the anti-war protest when he notes that "a different mood seems to be creeping into our politics:"

> We see a greater tendency to work outside of rather than through established channels, more demonstrations and fewer quiet remonstrances behind the scenes, a weakening of the traditional political parties as vehicles for managing conflict, direct action exalted and closed politics distrusted, a push for wider participation along with a vague feeling that government officials are aloof and no longer representative. The process is fed in some difficult-to-specify but important fashion by the electronic age media.

"Participatory democracy" in the movement is an organizational method deriving from the radical mystique of mass consensus. Groups and organizations are small, manageable. There are coordinating bodies (SNCC), local organizations improvised to meet local issues (WAGE), or chapters of national organizations (CORE). Built around the twin issues of civil rights and peace in Vietnam, the new movement is issue-oriented rather than doctrine-oriented. The organization that is a decentralized, literal democracy where "each counts as one," and where leadership cannot count more than rank-and-file members, is the ideal. This minimizes the role of leadership.

The problem, though, may be posed by the following question: Are the ideas of participatory democracy and community organizations compatible with the growth of industrialization and urbanization? "Elitism" and "indigenism" are terms which express the conflict over the role of leadership. What is more, flag burning and picketing seem to have entered the stage of diminishing returns. Shall the organizations adjust to loss of momentum and develop more centralized leadership styles of work or strive for mass participation which might lead to the same need in the long run? Also, how viable an alternative is pacifism—the leading "ideology" of the anti-war movement in the past—unless the issue is presented and perceived as clearcut and moral, like the war in Vietnam?

Direct action techniques, however necessary on pragmatic grounds, polarize strictly political goals. Further, is there such a thing as an anti-war "sentiment" merely awaiting organizing agents? Or is the anti-war movement a collection of groups and strata that must be carefully appraised for potential irritation with the going system? How can these issues be resolved "pragmatically" or by mere radical "oppositionism"? Furthermore, what should be done when opportunities arise within the going system to run for office or to serve as consultant to the forces opposed by the movement? Shall we join to be a constructive influence? Shall we preserve our moral purity as outsiders and risk utter loss? What good is partial reform? Without explicit ideological cohesion, can conflicts around leading personalities be contained? These questions are raised and disputed constantly.*

* The survey research data in this area are anything but definitive. Once the very general background variables (young, middle-class, irreligious, intelligent,

The intensity of this sort of political participation, demanding whole-hearted commitment and much time and emotion, makes it particularly unstable. The momentum achieved by high public interest, relatively broad participation, and the dramatic appeal of the "new" have conspired to submerge questions of organization and ideology. But whether or not this "moral style" of political action survives, politics in the age of mass participation will draw opposition. For the reduction of "political man" to "civic man" is intolerable to the romantic moralist unconcerned with the idea that in this "specialized age" radicalism is not "practical."

The anti-war movement can travel any one of three available roads. It will probably try to travel all of them. Yet if the movement is to find appropriate answers, it needs unfettered time. And the question thus shifts to whether the American political system, as currently structured, will permit the process of discovery, and later, of change, to be nonviolent.

The anti-war movement can take a place in the American party system only after very serious changes have been made in that system. Even if a major party officially adopted the goal of peace in Vietnam and achieved it, the movement would not be satisfied, given its present ambitious social goals, which include the formation of an international system for insuring world peace and economic development for the less developed nations. Although a large portion of the anti-war movement would be willing to accept the party system as the basis for a peace movement, a sizable sector of the current anti-war movement—that portion which sees the war

moralistic, etc.) are accounted for, there seems to be little that distinguishes the anti-war protester from peer group relations exhibiting the same cluster of variables. A recent interesting study has attempted to isolate the factor of nationalism, but the amount of explained variance does not permit much optimism for a refined universalist-particularist scale (cf. Stanley J. Morse and Stanton Pearlman, 1968).

system as endemic to the imperialist system—would not. That unwilling portion of the anti-war movement could press for participation in the politics of the working class. This would involve a search for new legitimacy along broad class lines instead of direct political participation along special interest lines.

> The phrase "most Americans" is rather deceptive at times because it obscures who is being talked about. Specifically, in class terms, "most" includes the strategic property-owning groups and their salaried personnel in the corporate economy; the managers, professional, technicians, and clerical forces. It includes the proprietary groups of independent businessmen, free professionals, and small farmers. It includes skilled, semi-skilled, and unskilled members of organized labor. It includes the black bourgeoisie and long-term employed black proletariat. It includes practically the whole of the clergy and the vast majority of students, black and white. It includes "womanpower" as well. The anti-revolutionary consensus is overwhelmingly sustained by traditional ethnic national groups, who can be relied upon to supply an initial striking force. The mass potential available for the support of a fascist counterrevolutionary move in the immediate period ahead is tremendous (Peck, 1968: 51).

The organized working class has become increasingly "non-violent" as it has been subject to all forms of organizational restraints—such as collective bargaining, labor-management arbitration of strikes, participation in investment programs, and the increasing importance attached to health and welfare benefits. Indeed, the working class has become functionally legitimized, with full recognition of this class by all other established sectors of American society. Portions of the unorganized lower class and the disorganized marginal class, not subject to any of these customary restraints, and not legitimated by the larger society, remain the carriers of protest behavior, or at least of activities indicative of a general rejection of official society.

The present hostility between the working class on one hand and the lower and marginal classes on the other is not simply a conflict between newly propertied unionists and the unpropertied, but more nearly the struggle between the last great sector of American society to achieve legitimation, and the first great sector of that same society to reject the very bases of legitimation that the working class fought so mightily to achieve. The very concepts of "law and order," and their moral counterparts, "civility and respectability," which the nineteenth-century middle classes employed to prove that the workers would never be fit to participate in either the economic or political benefits of the national society, have now been taken over by the working class with an unparalleled vengeance. The working class finds itself taking over the guardianship of the national ethic of bourgeois respectability that portions of the middle class (and of the underclass) are now willing to challenge. The sons and daughters of the middle classes find themselves victimized not only by the gendarmes who found the police force an agency of upward social mobility, but victimized in the bargain by that very ideology of a self-satisfied bourgeoisie that has lost its lust for achievement.

The further difficulty is that the American working class, in contrast to lower-class ethnic and racial groups, believes itself successful—and part of that success is continued support of the war, or at least of the World War III industries (cf. Horowitz, 1964: 110-120). The sharpened struggles between a conservative working class and a radicalized underclass are the most serious drawbacks to an anti-war movement based on class politics (cf. Rainwater, 1968: 28-46).

Although the section dedicated to a direct struggle against the social order as a whole is small, schisms are already apparent in it. These range from the least violent, who live communally the pacifist life and ignore the behavior of the larger society, to the growing number of practiced militants who are willing to fight police hand-to-hand or bomb the symbols of the Establishment.

Roger Hilsman (1962: 452-463) has provided nine broad conditions for the commencement of internal warfare. And although he had obvious reference to conditions in the "underdeveloped world," they deserve mention, if only to show how many of these indicators exist in the United States.

(1) Antagonism between underdeveloped states.
(2) Disagreements between regions of a state or between a region and the center.
(3) Intense disagreement over foreign policy.
(4) Traditional political rivalries within a social class.
(5) Social class antagonism.
(6) Lack of a popular belief in the state as a sovereign entity.
(7) Ethnic or racial issues.
(8) Banditry.
(9) Constitutional crisis.

If we substitute antagonism between local and national forms of authority, and a high rate of economic crimes, it is clear that the United States contains within its boundaries the basic ingredients of internal war. In this sense, the turn of the anti-war movement toward a more violent pattern may indicate a general crisis in legitimation—which is, after all, what these nine indicators are all about.

Social conditions for internal warfare may be present in America today, but the military logistics necessary for an effective insurrection are not. Even a remote chance of success requires (1) outside support of a military sort, (2) a severe internal crisis to shatter the confidence of large numbers, and (3) social unrest occasioned by an international defeat (cf. Gross, 1958). None of these exists today. Consequently, street fighting gains little; indeed, it gives military and paramilitary agents the opportunity to cripple resistance movements permanently.

A recent study by Martin Oppenheimer (1968) of paramilitary activities in urban areas outlined the disastrous failures of insurrectionary efforts in the cities of other countries and other times: the Dublin Easter Rising of 1916, the Shanghai Riots of 1927, and the Warsaw Ghetto Rebellion of 1944. More significantly, he indicated how in the absence of objective conditions for rebellion, the strategies of rebellion may boomerang.

> The dominant power structure can cope with paramilitary activity in a combination of two ways, similar in most respects to its strategy in any insurgency war. It can move radically to solve the problems of the population, thus cutting off the guerrillas' base of support in the populace, or it can move to suppress the military activity through counter-insurgency warfare and other military means—including aerial bombardment.

This seems far more typical. The liberal solution, attempting to combine these two strategies, is inherently inconsistent. Military force inevitably (in an urban situation particularly) injures the innocent and wins more support for local guerrillas. "The other war," that of reform measures, is in this way understood.

The officials of society must choose either a radical or a reactionary course just as do the marginal members. Insofar as choice still exists, it must be of goals as well as means and must be made by those on both sides.

Part II

The Message Is the Struggle: The Radical Pivot

AMERICAN RADICALISM
AND THE REVOLT 7
AGAINST AUTHORITY: 1950-1960

There is a "soul searching" dimension to this question: what is the relevance of a political minority? When asked, it usually carries the implication that the hearers should turn their eyes inward. But as I see the matter roughly formulated, the relevance of a political minority is the process by which it ceases being altogether a minority and becomes a majority, if not in vote-getting power then at least in popular sympathy. But as a matter of unfortunate fact, those who ask this question usually emphasize the phrase "political minority" at the expense of the word "relevance."

The years between 1939 and 1959 were filled with betrayal of radical causes, substitution of parochial and strident national interests for international values, and, most recently, with talk about the "end of ideology" in the West and the futility of a radical approach to political and economic problems altogether. In the United States, the old futilitarians joined forces with the new technocrats to deny the relevance, not simply of political minorities in American life, but of politics as such. In this context, it is little wonder that those in search of a radical polity have become introspective, introverted, and inhibited.

Nonetheless, the very failures of radical minority politics in the past should caution us not to attempt to reconstruct radical parties without a basic reconsideration of the contents and aims of relevant political behavior.

The foremost aim of all relevant politics must be to win—to emerge victorious—whether through electoral processes or through direct public persuasion.

It is no accident that the only sector of society in America which discusses the question in terms of minority affairs is the political "left." This is a consequence of the era of the thirties and the disaffections and disaffiliations of the subsequent decades. Such a mode of thinking carries an implied metaphysical pathos, as if a certain nobility accrues to being both a minority and on the Left. Of course, such a style of thought assumes the rightness of the minority perspective. There is a psychic dislocation—from a minority which *can* be correct to one which *must* be correct, by virtue of its "underdog" status. In relationship to the peace question, a "we and they" attitude of mind develops: "we" understand the costs of the arms race, the folly of the fall-out shelters, the danger of accidental wars; but "they" (meaning the vast majority of the American public) see only the benefits of the arms race, the pragmatic utility of fall-out shelters, and the impossibility, given the "padlocking" of thermonuclear explosives, of accidental wars.

Political minorities thus discreetly and almost without notice become transformed into a Platonic truth-bearing elite bringing the message of apocalypse to a public indulging in Roman orgies. Although there is no denying the possibilities of minority expression on a host of social and political questions, it has been both a folly and a danger to raise the matter of peace in such terms. The following series of propositions represents an attempt, therefore, to show the majority relevance of a thermonuclear pacifism.

1

The first and foremost premise is that our age is one which has transformed the fantasy of universal destruction into a hard reality. "Total solutions" are not just possible, but have been witnessed. Auschwitz and Lidice were the "first strike" of massive technological genocide; Hiroshima and Nagasaki bore the first bitter fruits of scientific annihilation. No questions were asked about what kind of Japanese citizen should live or die—the atomic bomb was nondiscriminatory. No one questioned what type of Jew or Czech should live or die—the gas chamber in this special sense treated all as equals. And the structure of nuclear weaponry is not of such a nature as to admit to such fine distinctions between military and civilian, majority adherents or minority deviants.

Despite the phraseology of "tactical" nuclear warriors, it has become increasingly evident that crossing the thermonuclear line would loose a holocaust that would violate all social and political distinctions. War is not an adequate term to describe the dangers of the current situation; in a war there are soldiers and civilians, front lines and rear echelons, victors and the vanquished. In nuclear warfare, these conventional distinctions no longer obtain, and it is of little purpose to speak of minority and majority perspectives. The new distinctions classify nuclear weapons by their death potential. The job of the "minority" of political literates is not to revel in superior wisdom, but rather to wipe out dangerous forms of ignorance about the current situation.

2

A second major reason for rejecting a theory of minority relevance is that the dualism between minority and majority has meaning only in terms of issues where a legitimate division of interests obtains. It is possible, and perhaps even necessary, for a healthy and vigorous society to exhibit sharp differences over questions ranging from the legitimacy of economic profit to the worth of marriage. For on such matters there are clearly defined "interests" and "attitudes" at stake. The interests of employees might be to maximize wages, while those of the employers would be to maximize profits; similarly, one might distinguish between those who see their "security" in the marital condition and those who see their "happiness" in staying unmarried. Here there exist legitimate grounds for debate—for minority and majority cleavages of opinions and attitudes. Yet why does the question of thermonuclear conflict prevent the usual distinction between minority and majority opinion? To ask the question is at least in part to answer it.

The function of war is the conduct of politics by "other" means. And politics implies differences of interests that entail the worth, if not the practicality, of solution. But in a universe of technological "overkill," war has become total, and hence harmful to everyone—at least insofar as we are speaking of thermonuclear war. This totality suggests a merger of interests and attitudes. The sovereignty of rational human interests takes precedence (and even makes possible) the particular social and personal conflicts of interest raging in the world. Peace at this juncture may well be defined as "planned conflict"—at least to the extent that a condition of peace is a necessary stipulation for all other divergencies of interests, and on all other matters of social, political, and economic relevance. Peace is not the "interest" of any one special group. It is the concern of the human group as such. Likewise, modern warfare no longer benefits some and endangers others; it threatens mankind as a whole. The argument for deterrence is based on a conventional theory of war, one that assumes the unitary character of all warfare and, hence, the relevance of spheres of "influence" and "interests."

<h1 style="text-align:center">3</h1>

The mobilization of widespread concern for the future, based on the public understanding of thermonuclear annihilation (which must necessarily include knowledge about the military minded—in and out of uniform), requires retooling and rethinking. It requires a retooling of the political parties with people dedicated to the principles of the party of their choice, people who see peace as a necessary undergirding for realizing those principles. It requires a rethinking of the foundations of the radical posture in terms of its historic deficits as well as its manifold successes. Peace is not a demand restricted to one social sector, or a monopoly of one party or one ideology. Therefore it cannot be legitimately approached as a problem in the logic of minority relevance. The radical group in the United States is comprised of old futilitarians, young turks, and a wide group of "middleaged" middle-range folks who are really fearful of the consequences of majority politics. The peace "movement" as it is presently constituted is to a large extent a convenient linkage of socialists, ex-communists, pacifists, utopians, and rebellious youth. As such, it does not so much constitute a "movement" as a loose group who want peace and possess common strategies.

It is to the credit of these "left-out" factions that they have the presence of mind to want to act in terms of what has been spelled out by the scientific and scholarly community. However, such a gathering as now exists amounts to a reconstitution of the *old* Left around the unifying theme of peace. It has not really penetrated the heart of the American consciousness far enough to be called, as it is in Great Britain, the New Left. Furthermore, even if such a New Left was to emerge in this country, to do so around the theme of peace would be both misanthropic and dangerous. It would convert the peace issue into a political party issue—a minority party question. It could decisively alienate entire sectors of American society so that peace would be considered partisan work. We do not want nor need a "peace party" competing with a "war party." We do need to make peace a universal human interest, a heartfelt common concern.

4

There is yet another sense in which talk about the relevance of a political minority has lost its meaning. The old radical minority lived in a reified world of capital versus labor, imperialism versus socialism, good Scouts versus bad Indians. The innumerable revolutions of our times have gone undetected, or at least been assiduously avoided by minority politicians. These are the ongoing revolutions in scientific production (automation); in techniques of massive distribution; in consumer-oriented consumption; in the social sphere, in the growth of urbanization and of the megalopolis; in the economic sphere, in the change-over from private to public sectors of ownership and industrial operations; in the political sphere, the shift from command structures such as Peronism, Hitlerism, Stalinism to consensus structures which now exist in both the United States and the Soviet Union; in personal ethics, from the traditional authoritarian family mold to the highly individualist and experimental personal patterns. All of these revolutions have so far not penetrated radical minority politics in the United States. Even to raise such matters is to risk the charges of academic obscurantism and Panglossian nonsense.

The "old radicalism" has become the "new conservatism." What we have gotten are essentially nostalgic yearnings for the simple "good-old-days" when a "union-man" could be distinguished from the "company fink." In contrast to this are those old radicals who, failing to "beat the system," have decided to "work the system." Still maintaining their socialist purity, they act as guardians of our virtue—making sure that revolutions around the world which deviate from the nineteenth century blueprints are properly condemned. The "official" socialist literature (e.g., *The New Leader*), is only ideologically distinguished from the "official" capitalist literature (e.g., *Fortune*). To become an editor of either side of officialdom has become the height of fashion in our age.

The old Left and the new Right both err in not recognizing that the world is in a state of intense social agitation precisely because the failure to share in the "new revolutions" of our century has come to define what we mean by "underdeveloped" areas. To maintain that the liquidation of the older problems has everywhere taken place is wishful thinking—a form of Establishmentarian celebration that only makes the old Left/new Right appear ludicrous in the eyes of the rest of the world. However, we are not herein concerned with the relevance of minority postures alone, but more particularly of radical minority postures.

What must be emphasized is the dismal failure of contemporary radicalism in America to understand the new revolutionary forces which exist. The crucial question for those who want to be both radical and realistic is just what is the point of crossover between present revolutions and inherited antagonisms. But precisely because radical currents in the United States have failed to come to grips with new social and scientific conditions, they as much threaten the search for world peace as enhance it. Old dogmatic ideologies and even older forms of political endeavor simply will not prove effective. Soap-box oration for peace would simply turn the peace issue into platitudinous sloganeering. Problems of decision-making and risk-taking, problems of the direct policy impact of strategically located people, problems of logistics and science are phases of the movement for peace that make it more than its converse, the peace movement.

5

Peace is everybody's business, for all people are in some sense "strategically located." We each function in a key capacity in some situation or another: as politician in relation to an electorate; as officer for the general membership in the American Legion or the Parent-Teacher's Association; as teacher in relation to students; or as administrator in relation to a factory line. The peace concern does not require us to abandon normal functions and proficiencies—to "surrender" professional competence, concern, or allegiance—in order to function in a "peace movement."

The problem of annihilation is a common interest and a common concern. Each person can illuminate it with his special knowledge and distinctive social roles. Thus, the physicist can describe the dangers of fallout and high megaton weapons. The chemist can examine the properties of radiation and its effects on the human organism. The sociologist might examine questions of social disorganization attendant on large-scale nuclear conflict. The psychiatrist can deal with potential effects of widespread warfare on personality and mental illness. Nor is this simply a "professional" or "academic" undertaking. The labor leader may inform his members that the "boom" of a war economy may lead to the "bust" of total destruction. The housewife can make clear her fears over the potential loss of children and the psychological hurt to her children in this present climate of "terror balances." The businessman can introduce questions of the loss of trade and markets brought about by a schismatic approach to nations of the world—divisions of East and West which are ideological rather than economic. In brief, peace is a common concern because the threat of human annihilation is a direct and organic challenge.

<h1 style="text-align:center">6</h1>

A deep tragedy in the present context is the separation, in the United States, of a good portion of the Left from the peace movement. The ossified battles over "Stalinism" and "anti-Stalinism" have driven a sharp knife into the remnants of the inherited American Left. The strange phenomenon has arisen wherein disagreements over the nature of the Cuban Revolution, the Hungarian Revolt, and the Berlin Wall have led to a virtual abandonment of the peace issue by the contributors to this somewhat furtive "great debate" in American radicalism. For the "outsiders," new to the peace effort, the fact that such disputations count for little, if anything, is simply discounted. And the dedicated peace worker may just as readily find himself denounced for aiding and abetting the cause of the Soviet Union by sections of the old Left as by sections of the new Right. It is not difficult to imagine that people who take peace as a serious and central concern of our times might be frightened away from further effort—if only to escape the torrents of criticisms from "insiders" as well as "outsiders." Present-day American radicalism has suffered and is suffering from the plague of Stalinphobia—the effort to settle the question of the Soviet Union *prior to* any efforts on behalf of settlement of disarmament between the great powers. As long as radicalism in America confronts the public with a choice—communism *or* socialism—it will remain part of minority politics. Perhaps most damaging, it would force a choice of social system and national interest when it is precisely such choices which fan the flames of the Cold War. The rise of an articulate minority knowing and skirting the dangers of Stalinphobia offers the best hope that the minority of today's peace forces will indeed become the majority of tomorrow.

7

However, there is a question of political minorities that is indeed pertinent, and all too rarely examined. For those who wish to make peace their paramount and everyday concern, questions of qualification, and of credentials, are all important. They may be concerned with peace as an outcome of the failure of past political radical movements, be involved with a peace movement as an ego-gratification in lieu of satisfactions of a more customary variety, be interested in peace as therapy for middle-class boredom—or for that matter, for working-class political messianism. But all of these are insufficient, either as credentials or as recommendations. The American public is rightfully suspicious of panacea-makers and self-styled reformers whose solutions are worked out in advance of everyday tough problems. The growth of a warrior ethos, the escalation of the arms race, the breakdown of the negotiation processes between the great powers—each of these took a long time in the making. It would be foolish to imagine peaceful accommodation and settlement evolving any more rapidly. Working for peace requires an abandonment of stereotyped thinking about "we and they," East and West, the United States and the Soviet Union. It requires an abandonment of traditional neo-Machiavellian political techniques of manipulating the peace concern to promote special interests which may or may not coincide with the general concerns of peaceful existence.

There are, to be sure, many fine and capable people in all walks of life dedicated to the search for peace. The peace entrepreneur must come before the public with a desire and a capacity to cooperate with all sectors of the American public: Democratic and Republican, black and white, labor and management, left and right and center, Christian and pagan. Only such a person can properly claim to represent himself as a relevant minority figure, for only such a figure can hold out the chance of widespread majority acceptance. Patience, competence, and organizational skills are virtues in any major venture.

8

What we now find in consequence of an exaggerated emphasis on the relevance of a political minority is a search for "pure" organizational forms, with "special" roads to salvation mapped out in advance. Distinctiveness is substituted for distinction and practical success. The forces organized for peace thus present a spectacle of many organizations with many leaders—but without mass membership. Apparently it is no longer sufficient to have "scientists for peace"; now we are urged to have "social scientists for peace." Likewise, it is no longer enough to have "women for peace," but we are now told of the "need" to have "children for peace" and "children's marches for peace." This minority thinking has several social sources: one is the strong anarchistic (read egotistic) tendency either to lead an organization or to leave it; another is an animus for the political Establishment and hence an easy transference from disliking conservative "inflexibilities" to rejecting such people as "disruptive elements"; last is the simple misanthropic notion that ongoing peace institutions—from the United Nations to the American Friends Service Committee—are not "militant" or "active" enough. All of this represents a concentration on self rather than on peace.

The same situation holds true in relation to publications. There exists a plethora of peace periodicals—redundant, poorly distributed, and often of inferior design and format. The fact is that opportunities for the peace forces to contribute to large circulation magazines and major scholarly and learned periodicals have never been better. But it is easier to start a periodical than to submit copy which may not be approved by an established board of editors. And of course it is easier to blame the "biases" of editors than to admit the possibility of shortcomings in literary form or in logical content. The successes of such men as C. Wright Mills and David Riesman and Seymour Melman would indicate that a large public is ready to purchase and sympathetically receive writings on conflict resolution and world peace.

The radicals in the peace issue have more of a posture than a position, for they believe themselves exclusive possessors of truth. The other points of view are seen below—and moving toward or away from—this higher truth. This syndrome needs to be broken if an effective (and hence radical) peace concern is to be transformed into peace activity. What is needed is not a multiplication of bureaucratic agencies, but a multiplication of human agents willing and capable to work for East-West negotiation, accommodation, and cooperation wherever they are located and within the social problems they must face continually.

9

The size of the undertaking should not be minimized. The tasks of majority interests are connected not only with the need for responsible criticism but, more significantly, with the preparation for responsible leadership—the direction of large numbers of people representing different social forces and political moorings. For such a role, many of the virtues of the "old revolutionary" are in desperate demand and short supply: self-sacrifice, dedication to principle, singleness of purpose. The newly-relevant peace advocate must also come prepared with a technical proficiency at least equal to that possessed by our new civilian militarists. The need for technical and professional skills must be wedded to the dedication which has been the traditional hallmark of radical minority politics. Only in this way can the vicious cycles of defeat and disillusionment sustained by American radicalism for the past two decades be decisively broken. For only in this way can the conventional radical minority postures be transformed into majority deliberations and concerns.

The irony of the nuclear age is the transformation of the individual's role in history. For the classic conception of the individual as a "moment" in historical time, the growth of thermonuclear armaments and the consequent expansion of risks, accidents, and caprice has reversed social forces. History has now become a "moment" in an individual's time. This is the main fact and should be the main focus of any politics of peace.

8

AMERICAN RADICALISM

AND THE REVOLT

AGAINST REASON: 1960-1970

The American sixties reestablished a new radical element
in society. And it has had a perplexing effect, partly because
the current radicalism resembles the *fin de siècle* nineties
rather than the proletarian thirties. Most people concern
themselves more with analogy than with history; hence radicals create profound national doubt. This is the first generation in American society, at least in this century, to combine
political radicalism with irrationalism. As in the age of Sorel,
reason has been displaced by passion. Without exaggerating
such similarities, it might be instructive to pay stricter attention to them. If the proper responsiveness of man to technology is to provide an awareness of economic change as well
as social purpose, the proper response to history is to provide
an awareness of the classical sources of resistance to change
and even the frustration of purpose. Here I shall focus mainly
on this latter social factor. Hopefully, the concerns of this
book will be better understood against this contemporary
background.

There are roughly nine areas of marked similarity between French social thought in the nineties and the present period in American social life.

1

Perhaps the most obvious, and for that reason, most elusive, is the stylistic similarity between the last decade of the French nineteenth century and the present period in America. The current style of radicalism is abrasive, physical, impatient, and eclectic. It reflects a concern with the exercise of will over those objective forces which may exist in the world. But what is involved in the radicalism of the present generation, as in the past, is not simply a reemergence of humanism.

The assertion of the priority of individual will assumes a strongly moralistic tone. The wills of individuals become objects to be mobilized into one total will. This moralistic style is a ready handmaiden to the "totalitarian democracy" that the historian Jacob Talmon spoke of. It is a fanatic attempt to impose a new social order upon the world, rather than to await the verdict of consensus-building formulas among disparate individuals as well as the historical muses. Neither history nor humanism—allowing as they do for fragmenting diversity in decision-making and implementation, and for the egotistical needs of political elites—bring all men forward in a unified approximation of total and ideal good. But since without history there is no memory, the Good Myth gets transformed into the Myth of the Good.

The emphasis on will is not simply an abstract stylistic response to determinism. Political life does not work in such mysterious ways. Quite the contrary: the reason the nineties of the past century and the sixties of the present century reveal striking similarities is that both rest on the *success* of industrial capitalism—its ability, then as now, to provide a measure of affluence for a large portion of the citizenry; to integrate a huge portion of the population into the going political system; and to provide multiple channels for expressing resentment, hostility, and special interests. Working-class mobilization into trade unions made nationalism important in the conduct of World War I; when the chips were down, being German or French counted for more than being a member of the working class. The continued ability of trade unionism to satisfy working-class demands has set up a condition in which class politics, at least in world affairs, hardly exists in the United States. In short, the resurrection of the Revolutionary Will, as an expression of the Social Myth, closely followed periods of solid economic achievement, rather than economic crisis, as was the case after the Depression of 1929. The asserted need for Myth shows an inverse correlation with the success of Reality.

2

In its more specific ideological form, the New Left and the *fin de siècle* Left are both revolts against Marxism as a scientific historiography, and its replacement with Socialism as a vision of the good society. As Sorel clearly perceived, Marxism combines the double strains of humanism and moralism along a horizontal axis, and history and action along a vertical line. He also perceived that the emergence of a victory of radicalism in the twentieth century would necessarily have to tread over the dry bones of the Marxist legacy. And if the decomposition of Marxism seemed to be a premature announcement in the form stated by Sorel, it must certainly seem so no longer. Within radical circles at present, there are continued discussions not simply of "revisionism" versus "orthodoxy," but of alternative options *to* Marxism no less than within Marxism. In this very fact, "orthodoxy" has been liquidated, not by a frontal assault on shaky tenets, but as Sorel said it would be—through the outflanking maneuvers of empirical science.

The victories that Marxism chalked up in the twentieth century were those which displayed the advantages of will over history. The pure Marxist celebration of determinism slowly ebbed—in the Russian Revolution of Lenin in 1917, the Chinese Revolution of Mao Tse-Tung in 1949, the Cuban Revolution of Fidel Castro in 1959. These shared the thin silver thread of high leadership quality, characteristic of an uncorrupted elite. The charisma both of movement and men took charge. These three revolutions were not predetermined, nor even largely determined, by the economic failures of capitalism. They emerged spontaneously, able to execute the will of the revolution in the present rather than await the somber and spurious judgment of objective forces.

In this sense, the very victories attributed to the Marxist legacy were perhaps the most devastatingly undermining aspects of that legacy. Castro did more to destroy orthodoxy in radicalism than a century of anti-Marxist critics, no less than the chiliastic historiography that goes with that orthodoxy. The Sorelian vision that it was not necessarily Marxism as a whole, but Marxism as a deterministic system of science that was "decomposing" was to prove accurate. What remained in Marxism was the hard kernel of moral purpose. Precisely this same kind of attitude seems to underwrite the writings of present-day French revolutionists such as Régis Debray, one of the genuine cultural heroes of the contemporary American Left. A certain amount of naïveté, indeed a skepticism about theory as such, seems almost charming in comparison to the rigors which Marxists and would-be "students of Marxism" had to endure in the proletarian thirties, in the era of Communist ideological power in the West. The triumph of Marxism as a myth, as a guiding sense of political purpose, rather than Marxism as a blanket science of society, has come to characterize the present generation of the American Left. In this transformation from science to myth—as pretense if not as fact—nothing seems more clearly linked to the New Left as an ideology than the *fin de siècle* irrationalist doctrines of Bergson, Peguy, Le Bon, and this earlier liberation from the rigors of systematic theory.

3

What flows from this myth is a concept of will opposed to organization, as purity of conviction is opposed to stifling rationalism. Whether it be the *Bourse du Travail* or its modern counterpart, the Alinsky Street Corner Club, what seems especially and acutely characteristic is a suspicion that firm organizational lines of authority enhance predetermined and unreal ends distinct from what poor people care about.

There is a strong impulse toward anarchism in this feeling that tightly knit organizations lead to trouble and are well outside the purview of true radicalism. At present, as in the *fin de siècle* (particularly the work of Roberto Michels on the oligarchical tendencies of all organizational life), there is a strong doubt that close organization contributes to victory. Even in successful revolutions, such as those of China and Cuba, there is a post-revolutionary insistence that organization connotes stifling rationalism. This may simply be a function of the continued survival of the men who made these revolutions. But even so, there is a growing recognition that the problem with revolutions is that they terminate. Then the problem becomes: Now what?

The word "organization" is used more in connection with bureaucracy than to express the worth of organization for the mobilization of men. But if organization is doomed, what then is the guide of the revolutionary cause? Here we come to the emphasis on will and on the person. Marx left an ambiguity in this connection, namely, that men make history but only in ways prescribed by objective circumstances. The ambiguity is resolved by emphasizing the former proposition, namely, men *make history*, rather than in terms of the latter proposition: *under certain objective circumstances.* Phrases in the Cuban Revolution such as "to be a revolutionary, one must make a revolution" indicate the strong impulse toward the role of will. Activism of the self-fulfilling prophecy type is characteristic of the present Left. It was precisely what one found as the main line of development in the work of Sorel and his colleagues.

4

The assertion of the primacy of will over organization has beneath it an assumption of the prime importance of the person over politics per se. The question for radicals is never simply one of organization or bureaucracy, which are often discussed simply as negative consequences of the revolution. The main question is the value of political organization in the life of society. Political organization and legitimizing formulas break down and require restructuring, by revolution or reform. Breakdown devalues politics because it subjects men to one pessimistic outcome after another, to one political scheme and ad hoc supportive apparatus after another.

Political pessimism tended to isolate Sorel from the euphoria of Socialist party activities of the late nineteenth century, just as it does the contemporary New Left from the dreary vertigo of political party life of the Communist Party in this decade. The discouraging cycle could be broken by keeping men spontaneous, functioning as individuals, united by social feelings and common interest, and not obstructed by "pulse-feeling" political mechanisms. Persons collectively associate more stably and satisfactorily through cultural commonalities than they do by adhering to the political requirements of an organized party. The guerrilla movement offers a magnetic model of the transformation of radicalism from a rational to a romantic doctrine precisely as military insurgency offers a style of life free from organized political machinations. Present-day unity comes from a common youth culture: savage passion, idealism, concern with goals rather than interests define the "new politics" of the New Left.

5

Some critics say that emphasis on personal will as against the objectivity of history leads to an irrational society relying ultimately on terror to maintain itself and a bureaucracy to perform its tasks. The response to the criticism is remarkably similar in Sorelian literature and in the writings of the contemporary New Left. Basically, the answer given is that therapy is more important than victory. Orientation overrides achievement. Passion and meaning in struggle are more valuable than material accomplishment. As bureaucracies favor the latter over the former, it is necessary to destroy them periodically, in order for purpose to reign supreme. This is more vital than any specific victory of the revolution since: (a) the ultimate contours of a future society cannot be predicted and (b) the victory of the revolutionary factions often turns sour for lack of an adequate psychology or an adequate therapy to restore human purpose.

Precisely this therapeutic concern linked men like Sorel with their latter-day "revisionist" counterparts, such as Adam Schaff and Herbert Marcuse. The main idea is simple enough. The purpose of revolution is to create a society which is better than existing society. On the other hand, because the result is hard to guarantee, the more proximate goal of revolution is therapy for the participants, the revolutionists themselves. Therefore, the true change, or the essential condition for dramatic change, comes not with the triumph of one class over another, or the victory of one nation over another, but with the victory of each revolutionary over himself. This feature of Sorelianism is perhaps the most deeply felt, if not necessarily understood, by today's New Left.

6

Individualism and intense personalism, in both Sorel's time and ours, prevent the notion of political bureaucracy from becoming too entrenched. But it does more than this. It confronts the *radical* notion of the mass with the *socialist* idea of class. Such a radicalism views the non-governing elements in society in terms of their potential unity rather than their fragmented identity. Seizing upon the common feature rather than disruptive detail is considered essential to the promotion of social unification without the organization normally required to coordinate disparate groups.

The language of "mass" confronting "elite" is elemental and conducive to moral passion over analysis of various modes of group domination or group interrelatedness. The idea of the mass, fuzzy as it would have seemed to the orthodox Marxist, appeared to have many advantages. Above all it allowed for the spiritualization of politics, for a messianic Great Leader able to dissolve the obstructions of class identities and speak directly to all people. The faith in the idea of the mass provided a radical glow to what otherwise may have appeared to be intensely individualistic and excessively conservative zeal for the Great Man. The mass is most purely itself without an urban overlay. Sorel emphasizes the pastoral values, the diligence and high potential of the peasantry for drastic revolution and social change. They retain an untarnished popular character and represent the real essence of Oppressed Man. The oppressed man is no mere proletarian. He may be a French peasant, a Roman Catholic leftist, a member of an ethnic minority or a radical cluster. This commonality is a social principle, the herd instinct in social life, a factor promoting contact between groups. Leaders are actually intensified cases of this elemental collective character in all men. To lead the mass no "vanguard" organization would do. The intelligent, courageous apaches alone symbolize the mass personality. Only they can concentrate their energies and liberate the herd.

Those who endow a "class" with historic responsibilities and charge men with enough analytic understanding and rational power to read historical law are declared the new utopians—even more contemptible than the original utopians —since they lack even the earlier vision of a good society. The Marxist hero is a teacher-organizer on behalf of historical law which he must unfold. He is a leading strategist of *class* war and imposes organization to win that war, to fulfill a class responsibility and destiny for social reorganization. But to irrationalist leftism, he is merely preparing another class elite for rule, failing to touch the real wellsprings of unity among men; he is a victim of the revolution he serves, which is both a Sorelian and a New Left concept.

7

Along with the idea of mass and the ambiguities of stratification as a mandate for revolution, there is the notion of conspiracy and the direct personal involvement in the revolutionary process. The notion of conspiracy is raised by Sorel, as it is now, not so much as an explanation for political problems or as a cynical response to the world. Rather, the idea of conspiracy assumes that politics is a consciously shaped process. Men who shape policy against mass interests find deceit a valuable political instrument. Yet they can be shown the errors of the conspiratorial theory and the dangers of corruption.

Fire can be met with fire. A conspiracy at the top may be toppled by a conspiracy from below. Popular insurrection can counter elite conspiracy. If elite conspiracy is supported by technology, particularly by computers that control and maintain information about all actors in a political system, it can be overthrown by a popular conspiratorial resort to the technology of direct weapons—firearms. If rulers conspire to deceive and solidify power by technological means, the unruly apaches, acting for the people, can conspire to undo them and make themselves effective by means of violence.

In this generation, political action has lost moral restraint in the same proportion as the political legitimation of the established system has lost effectiveness. The novel element in the political equation is not so much violence, then, as the sense of finally being liberated from inherited "bourgeois" restraints on both thought and action.

This neo-Marxist use of conspiratorial theory ascribes to rulerships a characteristic which is manageable by popular means or, even better than that, by a few actors representing a mass interest. Conspiracy can explain politics as a volitional network not subject to "inherent laws," a structure upon which the will can act, and, at times, act rapidly and decisively—perhaps with extraordinary results. Any young person can enter into a conspiracy rapidly enough, whereas electoral politics requires long-term visibility and mobilization. Conspiratorial politics is oftentimes extralegal politics, whereas electoral politics tends to be politics made, as well as defined, by lawyers. In this special sense, politics in the 1960s, as in the 1890s, was anti-intellectual; the focus was not on the forms of victory or on the quality of candidate, but on the substance of revolutionary conflict no matter how ugly or brutish the social ethics or personal style of the participants. Electoral politics always seems inadequate to overcoming the problems of industrial society and, in fact, often increases cooptation of newly mobilized social sectors. This leads one to suspect that advocates of conspiracy theory are less concerned with the goals of conspiracy than with providing a sophisticated antiseptic to those who participate in electoral politics.

It is not necessarily the display of raw courage that characterizes the nineties and today. Radicals of both epochs disdain certain kinds of violence, such as imperialist warfare. Rather, it is the personal absolution that one finds in the art of politics, and in the act of conspiracy, that becomes important, which makes politics therapy rather than the means to objective goals. In this sense, conspiracy theory, like political therapy, functions as a hedge against personal immorality. This deep fear of the political process as a corrupting element runs deep in the Left from Sorel to Marcuse and Goodman; and it also serves to distinguish liberal political goals from radical social goals.

8

Even before Trotsky, Sorel formulated the idea of the permanent revolution. He did so, however, not for the purpose of opposing an oppressive bureaucracy resulting from a totalistic revolution, but rather to accommodate the quest for change inherent in men and society. Even the best revolution consecrated to any single cause creates a basis for reaction and counterrevolution. It was necessary to conceptualize a means which allowed for change that would not undo the revolutionary victory at the start. Pioneer socialists, "Utopian" and "Scientific," and even the Russian Bolsheviks who followed them, tried to deal with revolution as an objective phenomenon subject to process and change.

Early Marxism and Bolshevism share an assumption that material changes alter personality. The latter adapts to the facts of the former. In this way it is claimed that socialism remains scientific and that the basis of socialist man is perpetually revolutionary. But in the *fin de siècle* interlude, certainly in the time of Sorel's criticisms of "scientific" Marxism, the mood was one of disenchantment with socialist promise and a search for its renewal. It was, in effect, both a demand that socialist man make an appearance irrespective of a socialist productive base and a willingness to speculate that maybe only some proto-socialist man could create a socialist base. *Fin de siècle* radicalism called for a reversal of causal estimates. A victory in the realm of psychology could take place despite what was occurring in the old, corrupt social order. Nor should this be thought of as simple impatience with history or the vagaries of social change. It became a matter of principle that a special kind of person was required to initiate revolutionary changes.

On this particular point the Sorelian idea links up dramatically with the neo-Marxism of the sixties, a phenomenon which also weathered disenchantment with old Marxist modes and apologetics, and with its organizational rationalism of the thirties. It too makes assumptions that the purity of personality, the change of life styles, or the redemption of humanity all could arise in any political order. The new key to transformation was sheer conviction. The very corruption of the old social order, whether or not it can be adjudicated, whether or not it can be reformed, should not limit the possibilities for personality development. Thus a renewed theoretical emphasis on will derives largely from this concern to bring about a revolution in the psychology of men as a precondition in society. And this meant in practice the liberation of radicalism from its own past taboos—sexual as well as political.

As it did in the *fin de siècle*, radicalism reasserts the priorities of egotism over socialism. For both, the body has a large vote. The main constituency of any social movement is the self. In this special sense, those in the New Left most attuned to the Sorelian moral vision are the so-called "hippies" or "street people," who, like Sorel, claim a powerful anti-political standpoint as a necessary basis for any psychological redemption or moral purification. Anti-politics becomes the essential cleansing agent of the psyche. Politics as candidacy and advocacy is, like Puritanism, a "hang-up" to be overcome, not a system to be worked.

9

The ninth point is also directly linked to the concept of the worth of individual personality. It took the form of a direct assault on the bureaucratic ethos, the administrative style of an organization. It is almost as if the individual, by his nature, contained a built-in resistance to organizational life, fearing its capacity to limit and circumscribe human behavior. The assault on bureaucracy, then, was not simply a reflection of anti-politics, either in the nineties or in the "swinging sixties," but a belief that acquiescence brings about impotence. The stultifying aspects of bureaucracy are widely known by liberals and populists of every sort. The essential difference for revolutionary leftists is that since a bureaucracy is an outcome of maintaining any social revolution which abolishes caretaker classes, it becomes a conservative and even backward agency unless men work against this tendency. The permanent revolution, therefore, has as its goal not only the salvation of personality, but its preservation from the organizational necessities of modern industrial society.

The similarities between the 1890s and the recent past extend to the belief that the revolutionary struggle is not seen as occurring between liberalism and conservatism but rather between radicalism and liberalism. The assumption is that under reformist pressures some variant of liberalism characterizes official politics. To revolutionize society it is necessary to combat the limitations of a liberalism now associated with official rules. Liberalism reigns in government. It has thus become a force against revolutionary change. It must be reconsidered as an impediment to social development. Liberalism does not, then, stand for a way of behaving politically, a mode of creative pragmatism. It is, rather, a reigning and now corrupt conviction.

The ferocity of the assault Sorel launches against the liberalism of his own age is thus theoretically as well as practically induced. For it was liberalism which became identified with the stultifying effects of reason and rationalized organization in society. It was therefore a challenge to liberalism rather than a challenge to knowledge per se that committed men like Sorel to an anti-rationalist posture.

This is also largely true of the modern Left movement, which is not so much an attack on the world of ideas as it is an attack on the idea that reason is the only mode of knowing. The suspicion is that reason is an ideology that teaches us to stand between two extremes, unable to act. This identification of liberalism with the spirit of judiciousness and prudence is precisely why liberalism, at the psychological level, continues to be the main target for radical jibes. It was the spirit of legitimation and juridical order itself which came under severe attack and reprimand. To attack the legitimation system of the modern Western world meant to attack the ideology of that system which had become and which remains the liberal ideology—an ideology no less elitist than the conservatism it replaced.

In noting major similarities which link the European nineties to the American sixties, at least from the point of view of what was going on in the world of radical behavior and radical thought, we must not forget the powerful and significant dissimilarities between these two periods.

First, the Sorelian *fin de siècle* vision was one in which the peasant and proletarian masses would become the spearhead of any revolutionary change. Sorel's class feeling firmly underlay his mass concept and remained committed to a Marxism, or at least a Bakuninism, which allowed the notion of revolution to take place outside a proletarian vanguard of "organizers." Sorel's vanguard retains psychological propensities to violence and irrationality which do not necessarily correlate with the stratification system. Nonetheless, the lower classes serve as the necessary agency of revolutionary change.

This is obviously not the case for much of the New Left. The new vanguard group, far from being the factory proletariat, is probably the educated sector of society most removed from processes of production. In point of fact, current radicals are partially composed of groups which Sorel and his colleagues considered corrupt, namely, the educated classes. This is largely because American politics is structured to assimilate generational surge as a source of change, its class structure being flexible enough to absorb such pressures. Generational discontent displaces class discontent because classes in American society are plugged into some scheme for sharing in the national wealth and supporting national symbols.

In an individualistic, competitive environment that demands specialized skills as a precondition for participation and advantage, the young are disadvantaged by the system to the extent of challenging it. The challenge may become simply another formula for including new groups, or a revolutionary alternative to the system. It thus becomes the young who are most difficult to assimilate and who are most readily alienated. The young become a chief source of challenge and innovation.

The difference between the present generation and the *fin de siècle* ideal is the breakdown of distinction among political marginality, deviance, and revolutionary behavior. Hero types are no longer proletarian or productive. They are virile, savage, angry, akin to a popular image of the black, the isolated youth. The educated have lost the tradition of lionizing the productive labors of worker and peasant. It is more important that hero types show authentic inner turmoil, political convictions unmitigated by the complexities of a relativistic and thus immobilizing education. As liberal, middle-class Left elements have moved away from achievement orientations (simply because their parents left precious little to "achieve"), they have lost a radical idealization of earthy labors and have instead idealized poverty as a "way of life." The poor were said to create superior conditions for cooperative community, for ethnic communication, and for personal identity. Class models for reorganization have yielded to racial-ethnic models. The radical young feel charged to revive these values and have in effect connected the "culture of poverty" with generational rebellion. Moreover, the "swinging style" of poverty "cultures" such as the black and Puerto Rican has a natural appeal to those youths searching out an uncluttered life-style.

A third difference is that *fin de siècle* radicals had a strong military commitment—a commitment to the use of violence as a purifying act while also a necessary compensatory device for the disadvantaged who reveal a lack of political organization. Elements among today's Left are diffused in pacifist and activist directions. Attitudes toward class wars are as negative as toward international conflict. Still, this is only partially characteristic of the New Left, which increasingly has taken a guerrilla "line" on black violence. Whether the martial spirit will be sustained in the future and become completely characteristic is difficult to predict.

For the *fin de siècle* it was still possible to have a martial ethic linked to a socialist destiny. In an age of super weapons the display of armed heroes is menacing in proportion to the technological destructive power at their command. The same capacity to exercise a radical ideology over a large group of people now demands a commitment to the idea of pacifism or at the least to the notion of international peace.

The main differences, then, are not so much ideological as they are functional. Successful revolutions in Russia, China, and Cuba indicate that the dialogue of the nineties was concerned with what would yet come to be. The dialogue of the present radical generation must always start from the fact that socialist revolutions have in fact succeeded. They are capable of pointing to pragmatic successes much in the same ways and in the same areas of production as capitalism. Radicalism is thus subject to the kind of withering criticism which Sorelians were spared, as they were concerned with the future and not with the defects of the accomplished socialist fact.

Our own times may show a radicalism which is more in tune with the irrational style than even the *fin de siècle*. The attack by the Left on society has become totalistic. It has joined political marginality to social deviance in ways thoroughly alien to Sorel and his age. It has become an attack on socialism as well as capitalism. It has become an attack on industrialism as well as agrarianism. It has become an attack on technological achievement no less than those who would engineer the soul. This kind of assault is atypical and uncommon even for the most violent proponents of the Marxist vision—orthodox or revisionist.

It is simpler now to argue a case for social radicalism as something apart from political revolution. In the nineties, the case for radicalism and for revolutionary politics was still inextricably linked. This very linkage is now threatened by withdrawal of huge portions of the under-class population from legitimizing the behavior of public officials. The problem of compromise plagues the radicals more today than in Sorel's time because accommodation has become the dominant motif of politics between nations no less than within a nation. This cannot easily be acknowledged, much less countenanced, by radical irrationalists.

What is to be found in the historical context is a coexistence over a long period of time between different social systems, their adaptations to each other and to unique circumstances. In other words, there has not been a historical displacement of one system by another, or one pure form of statecraft by another; rather, there has occurred the crystallization of new mixtures. Many similar ideological starting points take different forms in different nations, inducing similarities and differences unforeseen by political leaders—such as the fact that bureaucratic socialism in an East European country .may have as much in common with bureaucratic capitalism in a West European country such as France than either may have with the underdeveloped areas of the world.

The alienated sense of being extrinsic to power remains just as strong for the New Left as it was for the Sorelian Left. Socialism and capitalism continue to coexist in peaceful disharmony. So too do radical and reactionary demands for violence coexist in a form not too far removed from their *fin de siècle* formulation. Fascism returns in the United States not as a right-wing ideology, but almost as a quasi-leftist ideology, an ironic outcome that Sorel anticipated in his own writings when he celebrated Mussolini and Lenin as if they were really two peas in one pod. So has activism in America become neutral, a style used by both Left and Right.

FROM

9 TEACH-IN

TO MORATORIUM

The period from 1964 and teach-ins to 1970 and moratoriums might best be summarized as the transformation from the struggle as the message to the message of struggle. A brief characterization of that change may be useful at this point.

The fact that the war in Vietnam has remained a constant in the face of a tremendous growth in opposition to the war has led to an equally large-scale change in tactics and strategies. The assumptions of the anti-war movement in this sense have gone beyond what the leadership of that movement has either predicted or perhaps even desired. This is best indicated by the schisms and splits within the Students for a Democratic Society, particularly the emergence of a militant direct action faction called the Weatherman. Made famous in 1969 by a series of direct confrontations in the November 15 Moratorium and by a week of protest around the trial of the "Conspiracy of the Eight" (reduced to seven with the severance of Bobby Seale from the trial), the Weatherman faction accepts the use of counterforce, and even initiation of force, since force indicates a delegitimation of government as a democratic consensus.

At some point demonstrations must either cease as a result of real or symbolic federal pressures, or they must escalate. The Weatherman faction claims that the path of escalation is the only course of action that confronts imperialism directly and fearlessly. The Weatherman faction still confronts power as a Washington product—as central federal authority. It seeks to seize the reins of state power in a direct takeover of the Washington apparatus—apparently on the assumption that power in the United States is identical with the federal bureaucracy in Washington. Their tactical aspect aside, the desperation politics of the Left-wing in the Moratorium activities indicated a shift from a McLuhanism of the protest as the goal itself, to a Marxism of revolutionary struggle.

The other two anti-war factions most visible at the beginning of the seventies retain more symbolic and defensive approaches—essentially non-violent and legalistic. For the great majority, the revolutionary movement is the key element. The Moratorium was an expression of sentiment, based on the hope that such an expression would move the government to change its militaristic course of action. The assumption was that mass movements compel representatives to register protest. In this case it only led the president to call upon his silent majority—the majority that any president has in the midstream of a first term in office. Thus, the Moratorium movement propelled the mobilization of a counter-movement, and this had the effect of frustrating the purpose of the mass rallies. Instead of moving representative democratic institutions to the left, or to a peace position, it reinforced conservative trends following the presidential appeals for support.

The third faction stands between the large movement (Moratorium) group and the small militant Weatherman group. It is what might be called the political group. It is essentially a continuation of the 1968 Kennedy and Mc-Carthy wings of the Democratic Party. Many of the leading figures in the Moratorium are also involved in new Democratic coalitions and in the new politics in general. The position of the political group is that the Moratorium is not so much a reflection on the present state of affairs, but rather a statement of the future political coalition that will have to be forged if the war in Vietnam is to be brought to a satisfactory conclusion. In the Moratorium a large number of liberal Republicans were brought into play—such as Senator Goodell of New York—which gave a broader base to the political wing than party politics as such.

All three factions indicate a growing discontent with appeals to established political authority. But only the small militant minority is willing to defy the legitimacy system of the democratic process itself. This is significant, since the very praise the large majoritarian elements in the Moratorium received for being pacific in strategy and tactics served to alienate the peace movement from the system as a whole. But all three groups have run upon hard times: the Weatherman faction and other direct action anti-war groups are in a contradiction between a mass movement and minoritarian terrorism that isolates rather than integrates the peace movement. The Movement people remain many, but unformed. They hardly know where to go, and have yielded to other needs—environmental cleansing, population control, racial and community reduction of tensions, etc. In other words, the mass movement has no real ideological or organizational hold on its numbers. The political wing is embarking on a new politics. But no party lives on one issue alone, and no party is presently a peace party except in rhetoric.

But to leave matters at this level is to forget that the forces and factions which maintain the Vietnam war are stuck with the burden of using violence, terrorism, and genocide. The My Lai massacres underscored the absence of legitimacy of

the war and have served to underwrite the larger contra-
dictions confronting advocates of continued military hostilities—conditions that keep the peace movement alive even
against odds that might seem insurmountable on objective
grounds alone.

Thus, I shall devote the remainder of this final chapter to
the war question itself. The question of violence today cannot be seriously examined apart from the Vietnam struggles—
the very core of the issue of violence in America.

Robert J. Lifton has recently written in *Trans-action:*

> The Vietnam War, in its general social impact, has entered a new
> phase. It has become both boring and unmentionable. It is boring
> because practically everything that can be said about it has al-
> ready been said many times over.

In 1965, at the time of the first national Teach-In, the
United States had approximately 30,000 troops stationed in
that forlorn nation and a total casualty rate of 2,283 killed
and injured. In 1967, by the time of the May anti-war rallies,
we had approximately 375,000 troops under arms in Vietnam, a considerable number of additional troops in Thailand,
and a total casualty rate of 60,000. And by 1969, two years
later yet, the United States had approximately 500,000
troops under arms, and casualty figures had reached
135,000—including a death toll of approximately 17,500
men. This is surely a remarkable "timetable for withdrawal."
Nor should it be forgotten that soldiers are not the only
"casualties" in a war. Senator Edward Kennedy, who has
investigated the question, notes that as of 1967, Vietnamese
civilian casualties were occurring at the rate of 120,000 to
150,000 annually. But if one is interested in the total violence of this war, a look at the defoliation campaign, in
which chemical sprays are used to destroy productive acre-
age, should remove any lingering doubts. Chemical destruction has moved from 17,119 acres "treated" in 1962 to

843,606 acres in 1967, the last year for which such information is available. And we know that this figure has been steadily rising, since Congressional appropriations for chemical warfare jumped from $38.8 million in 1967 to twice that—or $70.8 million—in 1969.

If the acceleration of the war effort has been astronomical, then it must at least be pointed out that the rate of negative response has been equal to this challenge. The Moratorium represents the largest political strike in American history. And though elements in it may be opportunistic and perhaps insincere, this is a characteristic of all successful movements. They must necessarily attract a wide network of people, must become broad-based and must attract even fair-weather friends. For at this moment, all opposition to the Vietnam War is important in order to explain the scale of the anti-war movement.

The war has lost much of the intellectual rationale that it once had. Even such a hard-line organization as the RAND Corporation has witnessed the unique spectacle of its leading members arguing in 1969 on the need for an immediate ceasefire and withdrawal. The five points made by the RAND group in urging an end to the war provide a significant breakthrough in official thinking. I am taking the liberty of paraphrasing them because they reveal the extent of intellectual and organizational redefinition.

(1) Short of destroying the entire country and its people, we cannot eliminate the enemy forces in Vietnam by military means; in fact, military victory is no longer the U.S. objective. What should now also be recognized is that the opposing leadership cannot be coerced by the present or any other available U.S. strategy into making the kinds of concessions currently demanded.

(2) Past U.S. promises to the Vietnamese people are not served by prolonging our inconclusive and highly destructive military activity in Vietnam. This activity must not be prolonged merely on demand of the Saigon government, whose capacity to survive on its own must finally be tested, regardless of outcome.

(3) The importance to the U.S. national interests of the future political complexion of South Vietnam has been greatly exaggerated, as has the negative international impact of the unilateral U.S. military withdrawal.

(4) Above all, the human, political, and material costs of continuing our part in the war far outweigh any prospective benefits, and they are greater than the foreseeable costs and risks of disengagement.

(5) The North Vietnamese would never accept a settlement that "implied" recognition of the authority of the Saigon government. Thus to make the end of the U.S. involvement contingent upon concessions is to perpetuate our presence indefinitely. Withdrawal could even produce desirable political changes in Saigon by eliminating support for a regime not backed by a majority of South Vietnamese and by allowing a cohesive national consensus to emerge.

Why then does the war go on in spite of a divided public opinion and a bankrupt set of policy-makers?

First, no real ultimatum has been issued by any nation. Neither Washington, nor Moscow, nor Peking really demands an end to the war. No country really knows what to expect as a consequence of such a termination, and none is willing to run the necessary risks to find out. Neither the socialist allies nor the capitalist enemies of the Vietnamese people are willing to demand an end to the war. For all concerned, the war is good to the last drop of Vietnamese blood. The Vietnamese War is, after all, like a medieval war: well-programmed and firmly restricted in its scope and in its hardware. Thus, in some measure the war serves the interests of all three major parties to the Cold War. The United States can pursue its policy of international containment. The Soviet Union can legitimize its own adventurisms in Europe with impunity. And the Chinese can keep the United States military establishment pinned down as it copes with its own internal stresses and strains.

Second, the United States military network—which some may refer to as the military-industrial complex—can legitimize its position only through the continuation of the war system. We should not forget that more than 50 percent of the federal budget and 12 percent of the Gross National Product are directly or indirectly related to the war effort. And whatever overall benefits might accrue to United States industry as a result of a settlement in Vietnam, the selective disadvantages to the military system and the applied war-production agencies move to prevent any thirst for settlement on the part of the wealthy classes in America.

Third, if the military as a whole favors continued hostilities in Vietnam, American industry in part favors continued hostilities: many so-called World War III industries have never had or known peacetime bases—hence their strong fears of peace. Firms like McDonnell Douglas, Lockheed Aircraft, and Sperry-Rand are deeply locked into government contracts for military purposes, and hence believe their futures are mortgaged unless the war, or some worthy surrogate, continues. Thus, even though economists are correct in noting the overall profitless nature of the Vietnam War, the selective profitabilities help to keep the war machine going.

Fourth, the above should be coupled with a general absence of any overall planning for world peace. The United States in effect has been at war since 1940, since the lend-lease period and the lifting of the arms embargo to England, and the general military mobilization that commenced with the draft. Today, in 1970, we find ourselves saddled with these inheritances, and no equivalents. Urban programming has been sporadic and slow, and mobilization of wartime industries for peacetime capitalist competition has been even slower. Such inheritances as the draft conscription remain effectual even if the General Hersheys are no longer enforcing them.

Fifth, it should not be forgotten that the period between 1939 and 1969 has—with several crunches and lapses—been the most prosperous in American history: the university and college population has grown from one million to eight million (largely on the support bases of federal expenditures for education and research); the trade union movement has consolidated its position in the American economic hierarchy, so that while the movement is no bigger in numbers than it was thirty years ago, the power and prestige of its labor bureaucracy has grown immensely. The struggle for hours and wages has largely been displaced by a struggle for health and welfare measures—itself something tying the working classes to the war machine, by making job security and employee tenure the key issue, and preventing any wider vistas on their part.

Sixth, the Vietnam War must be seen, above all, as the residue of the Cold War. United States involvement began during the Cold War days, and it continues to express the anxieties and fears of that earlier period. In common parlance: "If we don't stop the Reds at Hanoi, then we will have to make a stand at San Francisco." The fact that the guerrilla struggles of war opponents in the Bay Area are directly linked to the continuance of the Vietnam War seems to have escaped the attention of the prophets of international Red conquest. The political leadership in Washington grew up in the Cold War atmosphere. Nixon, Laird, Kissinger et al. are heirs of those leaders who believed in and applied the Red-menace theory of international relations.

Seventh, there is the United States' tradition of war, a tradition that goes back two hundred years. The idea of losing a conflict has become anathema in the United States. Even sophisticated spokesmen speak timidly and soberly about how the fall of empires is determined by the passive acceptance of military defeat. For older civilizations like those of China and Russia, the idea of defeat is interwoven with the idea of survival and national integrity. For the United States, the only valid model seems to be England and France and other former European colonial powers. But even if such a narrow perspective were accepted, the United States would have an indefensible position, since the end of England's colonial position in India by no means meant the end of her economic penetration. Similarly, France retains a lively role in the economic expansion of former African colonies such as Algeria. And Japan, which lost its war thoroughly to the United States, has emerged as a leading power if not *the* leading power in Asia. It is simply about time for Americans to recognize that defeat in Vietnam will not mean the end of the United States' international power.

Opposition to the war has grown in numbers and in intensity. No more than two years ago, two-thirds of the American public supported the war effort; two years later the same heavy percentage oppose the war. What accounts for the change?

One: The rise of an articulate student subclass able to function as a mobilizing force on the campuses of America. The inequities in the system of drafting young men have played a particularly vital part in keeping opposition to the fore in the minds of young Americans.

Two: The rise of internal strains, particularly as they relate to the inability to find integrationist and passive solutions to the historic exploitation of the blacks. The rise of militant responses to the racist inheritance also means that blacks refuse to serve as a battering ram for the war effort in economic terms, that is, they refuse to be left at the low end of the wage scale. Thus, by whatever tactic and at whatever level, the Black Revolution in America has generated a two-front war—a dangerous situation that cannot be disregarded; and one that cannot be assuaged by symbolic concessions such as permitting black troops to go into battle with their hair "natural."

Three: The disintegration of the savings and economic position of those who in the past derived measured benefits from the war effort. The inflationary spiral has placed the American working masses in a bind: guns *or* butter has become the issue, rather than guns *and* butter. Personal savings are down, personal loans are up. Price increases follow in hectic pursuit of wage increases to sour the working people in this country on the war effort. Nor are these economic burdens felt only among working people. Middle classes too are polarized and fragmented by impossible tax burdens, and by the insecurities of their position vis-à-vis large-scale manufacturing and industry. Thus, just as there is selective support for the war at the producing level, there is a parallel selective position at the consumption level.

War is the science of violence. Thus war and forms of violence are inseparable as choices for conflict resolution. The scale of violence is trans-national. It involves nations as well as men, systems as well as pathologies. The rise of free-wheeling, violent groups on the Left is often, if not invariably, a response to the failure of responsible groups advocating law and order on the national scene to adhere to similar principles at the international level.

The ultimate irony is that groups advocating law and order are at loggerheads precisely on the dimensions at which they wish to consider problems of law and order. Conservative groups want to stamp out violence in the black ghettos of America, while radical groups want to stamp out violence in the swamps of South Vietnam. What emerges as the central fact of our age is that violence is indivisible. It will either spread or be eliminated in a context that is both national and international—encouraging a shift away from the unthinking acceptance of violence as the essential strategy for victory, no less than the determination of right and wrong.

It is often argued, and indeed persuasively, that violence is simply the price paid for certain goals, whether these goals be radical ones within the domestic context or conservative ones within a wider foreign policy context. When this is the case, the choice of struggle will be determined by the values held supreme, and not by the tactics necessary to gain those values. The problem with this sort of realpolitik formula is that it rarely if ever takes seriously the problem of violence itself. That is to say, there is a point of destruction reached which transforms tactical considerations into ultimate consideration. Otherwise, every form of fanaticism will be able to justify its own exaggerations in the name of democracy, national liberation, or any other current slogan of the times. The argument raging over violence is indivisible because the consequences of violence too often lead not to the anticipated or desired change in the social order or in the personality system, but to the no-win mutual destruction of antagonists.

Thus, either a consensus against the war in Vietnam or strife in the American ghetto may as readily focus on "tactical" considerations of violence as upon "principled" considerations of the purposes of insurgency. There is a sense in which the large-scale escalation of violence has called into question the character of current social conflicts. In so far as the purpose of all political struggle is some sort of social reorganization called "victory," the technological levels of violence tend to blunt any decisive results. If this were not the case, pacifism would be outflanked at every turn by militarism.

The blind adherence to struggle as an ultimate value must finally yield to a consideration of the forms of struggle appropriate to a world that can be destroyed in the name of noble sentiments and even healthy instincts. Thus it is that the issue of violence must be confronted directly as a social problem in itself, no less than as a consequence of other interests and values in conflict. For when all is said and done the resort to violence—to politics by "other" means—in fact implies the breakdown of "standard" means. And insofar as all social science is involved in the extended use of reason in society the social function of social science is linked to the conduct of politics and against the violence of conduct.

CONCLUSIONS

10 AND

CONJECTURES

The main conclusions, derived from an examination of all available information relating to anti-war demonstrations and anti-war sentiments in the sixties, are as follows:

One: The anti-war movement is basically in the hands of white liberals and radicals. This has become the main vehicle through which student movement activitism has distinguished itself politically from the earlier days of white involvement in black freedom struggles.

Two: There is an inverse correlation between organization and violence. Where there has been a high degree of organizational skill and attachments, there has been a much lower propensity for violent response. A great deal of violence is linked precisely through the loose organizational forms currently extant in the anti-war movement.

Three: Insofar as there is any violence in the anti-war movement, it is usually directed against property rather than persons and also the attacks are on state and government

114

property—such as ROTC buildings—rather than personal property as is characteristic in black ghetto violence. Police response has been to defend property by attacking persons. In this way the circle of violence is complete.

Four: Most of the violence is externally generated by pressures upon the law enforcement agencies to keep greater law and order and very little is initiated from within the anti-war movement as such. In fact, their is evidence to indicate that the anti-war movement has an extremely difficult time accepting violent forms of behavior or retaliation. This itself has occasioned rifts and even ruptures between orthodox anti-war movements such as SANE and the more unorthodox tactics employed by the participant groups in the National Mobilization Committee.

Five: The natural history of violence in the anti-war movement most often involves confrontations over symbols, such as beards, flags, and styles rather than over the exact issues involved in any specific struggle. The evidence would indicate that the gap stylistically is much wider than ideologically between the contending forces involved in demonstrations.

Six: While the anti-war movement often imitates many tactics of the black liberation movement, the former is clearly concerned with issues of legitimation and alienation, whereas the latter is concerned with problems of integration and increased participation in the benefits of American society. This, coupled with the surge of black nationalism, serves to sharply distinguish the forms of black and white left-wing power in American society.

Seven: The current movement against the war is not characterized by the factionalism of inner party disputes of the old Communist Left, but rather by fractionalism, that is, the conscious fragmenting of the anti-war movement into small nuclear cells, some linked to the anti-draft movement, others linked to the Vietnam conflict, and yet others to religious opposition to war in general. Each of these units tends to be responsible to no higher authority than its own immediate and often transitory membership, and each of these nuclear forms is potentially volatile for precisely the reason that there is an absence of organizational constraint or ideological restraint.

Reducing violence within the anti-war movement, insofar as this violence is occasioned by the movement, can only be accomplished by incorporating the largest possible numbers of participants into some aspect of legitimate political activity. For this to be successful there must be no identification of participation or of incorporation into the political process as a process of co-optation, nor a demand by authorities for the protesters to sacrifice participation to parliamentarianism.

In short, the anti-war movement started as a *reflex* to the larger international dilemmas in which the United States still finds itself, but it has evolved into a *stimulus* for precisely such dilemmas.

The curious and bitter irony is that after two world wars and two additional undeclared world wars against underdeveloped nations, we have now come full cycle: the ideologies of Left and Right have partially coalesced into a general assault on the present moment in history. Activism itself has become a style which is remarkably neutral and employable by Left or Right. In the larger sense, all political behavior has become "extremist"—that the Left has partaken of this bitter harvest is only a reflection of the larger failure of any American political culture to make a convincing case for total participation in the "system."

The conclusion to be drawn from all available evidence is that a moral choice must be made—by federal officials, local law enforcement agencies, political party workers, radical protesters, marginal social groups, and racially-oriented property holders, among others. That choice is either the democratic state or the garrison state. The conservative canard of "law and order," the genteel rubric of "justice, law, and order," the pieties concerning man's inner propensity toward destruction, the counterpieties of man's inner propensities toward self-destruction simply disguise the large-scale redivision and realignment now taking place in American society.

Perhaps George Wallace and the ultra-conservative movement he leads understand the current realities better than the traditional politicians or even the professional experts of the New Frontier variety. This nation is in a condition of polarization, not pluralization. The choices under such conditions become severely circumscribed. There can be either full participation of blacks in the affairs of Washington or fifty thousand National Guardsmen to escort five hundred thousand federal employees to and from their offices each workday morning and evening. There either can be full participation of young people, minority groups, and radical ideological spokesmen in political party conventions, or every convention held will require a detachment of counter-insurgent shock troops knowledgeable in the fine art of building barbed wire fences. It is not that these either/or propositions are the only available scientific choices, but rather that a large portion of the American population has come to expect, if not demand, a showdown over national aims.

No one should ever doubt that a society of law and order can be built. The historical evidence is clear that Germany under Adolph Hitler and the Soviet Union under Joseph Stalin had less "crime in the streets" than did the Weimar Republic or Russia during the Constitutional Duma. Penalties for stealing a sack of potatoes can be fixed at one year imprisonment per pound stolen. Consequences for mass demonstration against questionable foreign policies can be pegged so high that demonstrations will, in fact, cease to be a viable instrument of participation. The real question is: Does the price of gaining law and order exceed the social value received? This is where real "cost-effective" planning is required. For the price so far is the totalitarian society. The current wave of right-wing populism indicates the existence in American society of a large portion of the citizenry who in fact believe that the defense by authorities of their property values and their ideological values is indeed worth any price. To ride the hobby horse of a non-violent nation, however, is to run the risk of social stagnation and repression. It is to defend what the "haves" have, and to stand fixed against what the "have nots"—both political and economic—want. And the perimeter of that defense can extend from Dak To to Detroit.

The classical American style, the pluralist solution operating within the civic culture, is to strike a balance and an exchange between the haves and the have-nots, between the claims of the present and those of the future, and between a defense of nationhood and the legitimate restraints individuals put upon the nation (not to mention the demands of other nations upon our nation). In this regard, the advice tendered by Harris Wofford (1968) should be seriously listened to.

> I hope we pursue what Justice Fortas calls "an alternative to violence." This is law. But a lively, responsive law that is derived from the consent of the governed, that has reason as its central principle, that includes as part of the law's reasoning process the practice of civil disobedience. This new law, that I believe is promised by our Constitution, would prosecute and punish violence and lesser crimes; and it would distinguish between violence to persons, the highest kind of crime, and destruction of property, and there too, between actual destruction of property such as arson, and invasion of property rights such as sit-ins; and the last thing we would do is to invoke mass police action that involves the use of tear gas, blackjacks, clubs, mace or guns. The sad lessons of escalation in violence should be as clear at Columbia as they are in Vietnam.

One serious, even misanthropic, error made by conservative politicians is the implicit assumption that law and order are necessarily consonant with lower amounts of violent behavior. Experimental evidence would indicate that insofar as law and order is a surrogate for obedience, it promotes high degrees of violence. The work of Milgram (1963, 1965) and his associates indicates that while people expressed deep disapproval for administering high voltage shocks to others, and while some decried the senseless and stupid nature of committing violent acts against innocent victims, a large number of subjects complied with orders issued by experimenters. In practice, many subjects administered the most extreme shocks available when commanded by others willing to assume "responsibility." For some individuals, the experiment provided an occasion for aggressive release. If this experimental situation is placed in a macroscopic natural setting, it indicates that an excessive amount of conformity to law and order may have a boomerang effect—specifically, the readiness of large numbers to engage in punishing acts of violence at the behest of a leadership obsessed with following all regulations.

It must be said by extension that the destruction of the anti-war movement—whether in its abstract, universalist, and pacifist form, or in its nasty, brutish, and opportunistic form —would represent a far greater loss to the integrity of American democracy than any silence in the streets of our major cities or quiescence in the student centers in the hubs of our major universities. For obedience is not tranquillity; seething heavily is not the same as breathing easily. The anti-war movement has indeed caused disruption in governmental operations, increased the costs of domestic military preparedness, stimulated disaffiliation from the major parties, and been a general nuisance for an already burdened police force. But these are costs that can be borne by a society still capable of distinguishing between national concern and national celebration.

Let those who want law and order (of whom there are many) as well as those who want lawlessness and disorder (of whom there are few) weigh carefully the premium price that must be paid for the punitive state, in which the rage for order displaces the rationality of innovation. That price is the militarization of the United States of America.

TESTIMONY
ON 11
VIOLENCE

The following is a transcript of the hearing held by the National Commission on the Causes and Prevention of Violence in executive session on October 23, 1968. Chairman of the commission was Dr. Milton S. Eisenhower; other members were Judge A. Leon Higginbotham, Jr., The Honorable Patricia Harris, The Honorable Philip A. Hart, Mr. Eric Hoffer, Mr. Leon Jaworski, Mr. Albert E. Jenner, Jr., and Dr. W. Walter Menninger. Present also were Jerome H. Skolnick, Director of The Task Force on violent aspects of protest and confrontation, and Commission Officer Thomas Barr.

Higginbotham: I believe we are ready to proceed in executive session.

Eisenhower: Well, as I understand it, this was to be a round-table discussion rather than a presentation.

Skolnick: Gentlemen, Professor Horowitz is a professor of sociology at Livingston College of Rutgers University in New

Brunswick. He is the editor-in-chief of a magazine called *Trans-action* which is a social science magazine that is directed toward a more general audience than social scientists. He is also a consultant to this task force and has been working particularly on the anti-war movement. We thought it would be useful if he were to present briefly some of his conclusions and then we could have a discussion of his conclusions in the light of the testimony presented today.

Higginbotham: Thank you, Professor, and I just want to make one comment which I hope our staff will understand.

As a young lawyer, an old judge said to me that there is one thing you have to remember, that the brain cannot absorb what the seat cannot endure. (Laughter.)

We have been sitting for quite a long time.

Horowitz: I share your sentiments if not your seat. I have been here all day as well. In fact, I am glad I was, not necessarily for the learning process only. It strikes me that there are a number of occasions during the day's proceedings where I personally felt, and shared the agony, not necessarily over questions of inability to articulate to the fullest the character of the peace movement but a more profound agonizing, perhaps, that Senator Hart and Mr. Jenner and others kept pushing toward the question of goals.

One point of view involved here is an historical observation. Perhaps it can be viewed as a matter of the Old Left over and against the New Left. If you ask a member of the Old Left what his goals were, he continues to live in a pristine age where aims were very well-defined and socialism was a goal. There was much talk about the social and economic consequences of behavior and much more talk about the political consequences of behavior. One of the anomalies of the present (and it is not the fault of anyone who spoke) is the breakdown of these goals. One can't have the same attitudes toward the communists now as one did after the

Bolshevik Revolution, when all shortcomings were viewed as experimental lags rather than structural defects.

One of the real dilemmas involved in the movement is that violence may very well be a consequence of the frustration and aggression hypotheses. There are enough mistakes being made in order to implement anti-war goals to insinuate a certain amount of violence, not as violence, but as therapy. The therapeutic values that I dealt with in my report are key factors in defining the New Left. We tend to forget the compensations involved in this therapeutic view of violence on behalf of a long-range achievement of peace.

The major conclusions that I have arrived at—and I worked this material over for the last four months—are simple. Many of you have perhaps included them yourselves in your own calculations on violence. I think, however, they are worth mentioning, if only to point up in a preliminary way where we now are at.

The first point is that the anti-war movement is basically in the hands of white liberals and white radicals. This has become the main vehicle through which student movement activists have become distinguished and have distinguished themselves from the earlier days of white involvement in the black movement.

This has been reflected today in testimony, and yet perhaps there is a lack of candor to state frankly that the anti-war movement and the black liberation movement are indeed very different political commodities right now within the framework of radical America.

The second point, and I alluded to it in my preliminary remarks, is that there seems to be an inverse correlation between organization and violence. Where there is a high degree of organizational skill and detachment, there seems to be a much lower propensity for violent response.

A great deal of violence within the anti-war movement is hinged precisely to the loose organizational forms which are currently the fashion in the anti-war movement. You had a very good indication of that if you contrast the testimony provided by Mr. Sam Brown in the afternoon and the testimony of Mr. Tom Hayden in the morning. They are really quite different in the implications involved in their remarks and I think that, considering Mr. Brown's high degree of organizational commitment to politics, a very different set of parameters are at work than are at work in the testimony provided by Mr. Hayden.

I don't think it is only a question of attitude toward Senator McCarthy's campaign, but a general orientation toward organizational forms of behavior that distinguishes political from anti-political advocates of a withdrawal policy for the United States.

A third point in the findings is that insofar as there is any violence in the anti-war movement, it is usually directed against property rather than towards persons. And even then quite sparingly. I have Mr. Skolnick to thank for making a further distinction that these attacks against property are directed toward state and government property such as ROTC buildings rather than personal property of the sort that is characteristic in Negro ghetto violence. The anti-war demonstrators are not stealing televisions or looting small commercial enterprises. And I continue to believe that the distinction between the attack on types of property is significant.

At the same time, in this connection we have to recognize how important the value of personal property is in the minds of ordinary policemen and for the ordinary citizen. They are imbued with the importance of salvaging property. There is a kind of treadmill arrangement. There are attacks against property followed by police attacks upon persons. This creates a cycle of phenomena and makes it extremely difficult for us to weed out the sources and the causes of violent behavior, no matter how much factual information is at our disposal.

Fourth, most of the violence is externally generated by pressures upon law enforcement agencies to crack down on militants, particularly in a wartime situation—and very little violence is initiated in the anti-war movement. I refer to earlier testimony as evidence of this fact.

Jenner: Would you mind returning to your second point for a moment, as long as this is a roundtable discussion.

You seem to isolate attacks on personal property as distinguished from attacks on person in connection with the Vietnam war, the war issue. Certainly in some of the university eruptions of disorder, there have been attacks on personal property, haven't there?

Horowitz: Well, not really. There have been take-overs of buildings, but these were transient; and with a great show of deference for property rights.

Jenner: Well, they destroyed, for example, some doctor's twenty years of research, didn't they?

Skolnick: It was a professor's file and who destroyed it is unknown. But I think the general point Horowitz makes is correct, that the attacks on property within the university have been on a kind of quasi-public property. That is, these haven't been attacks on property for gain, but they have been rather symbolic attacks of the taking over of Grayson Kirk's office, this type of thing, purely a symbolic attack rather than an attempt to make oneself richer by stealing Grayson Kirk's armchair.

The distinction is important because the anti-war movement is such a symbolic movement and many of the responses on both sides, as Professor Horowitz will testify, can be seen as responses to symbolic events.

Now, we are not deciding here that it is good, bad, or indifferent, but we think it is analytically important to make that distinction.

Jenner: As part of the movement or protest, there has been, for example, the issue of exploitation of the disadvantaged in slums and ghettoes and the seeking of upward movement in society itself. There has been destruction of property.

Skolnick: I think one of the kinds of distinctions that we feel we have to make is between the anti-war movement, which we see sociologically as a white and middle class movement, by and large, in which the black communities have participated only peripherally, and ghetto protests. I think while there is sympathy and a rhetoric in the white group, and you heard Sam Brown, for example, talk about it, and there was, let's say in the early sixties, participation by white students in the civil rights movement, I think that the movements are clearly separable and use different tactics and have different kinds of results.

The white movement is a far more—so far has been a much more symbolic kind of thing, whereas the uprisings in the ghettos, many of them have been occasioned by two sorts of things: one, police activity, and the other, you can see, in the activity of the people in the ghetto, a response to the very serious economic deprivation that is felt in the ghetto.

Jenner: All right. Pardon the interruption.

Horowitz: That is perfectly all right. That obviates the need for any further explanation and allows me to get on to the fifth point, which is precisely the question of confrontation over symbols, beards, life style, rather than any specific economic issues involved in struggle.

From the evidence that I have, there is a much wider stylistic gap than there is an ideological gap between contending forces. I get that impression even from listening to the interchange between the commissioners and the panelists today. If there were only a way of stylistically communicating, ideological issues could be explicated and even adjudicated more easily.

Harris: Do you perceive this seizing upon the use of Anglo-Saxon monosyllables a question of style, an attempt to force upon the adult world a notion which the adult world resists and thereby gets involved in things which have no substance whatsoever?

Horowitz: Well, style in a certain sense is very important and has many substantive properties that we don't easily perceive.

Style is the substance of the generational struggle in a sense. The way one answers and the way one behaves and the kind of language one uses, which begins covertly as a matter of style, may very well end up involving matters of substance, although the direction that it takes may be unknown and unclear.

What we are involved with in the question of violence is also a matter of style. Violence can be perceived—you will pardon the expression, Mr. Hoffer—as an intervening variable. Maybe what we are really studying is not violence; maybe violence is a consequence of the kinds of problems that are raised by generations that may themselves be problems of style.

I am not entirely clear on this myself but I think it is worth looking into much more deeply than in the past.

Barr: I was amused at the brief interchange that I had with Hayden. I thought it was interesting, one, that he wouldn't play my game. I thought it was interesting that he wouldn't take me on the level that I wanted to take him on.

I thought it was also interesting that he had taken advantage, very cleverly I think, of the generation gap in being able to be flip and irrelevant in a very humorous way; I find that this content of the anti-war movement that relates to humor is something that older people are beginning to realize and take very seriously and they take it as a way of putting on older people.

Harris: Like Tom Lehrer. The use of humor by people concerned with very serious matters is not unique to this generation. And I must say that Tom Lehrer is the epitome of this kind of thing.

Higginbotham: For the record, the question has been raised by the acting chairman since the chairman is not presiding, who is Tom Lehrer?

Harris: Tom Lehrer is a former professor, I think at Harvard or Yale.

Skolnick: No, he was an instructor in mathematics who turned to music.

Harris: Who turned to music to satirize very cleverly matters of very significant concern from water and air pollution to the song that most of us have heard, "We shall all burn together when we burn," which is his approach to the problem of the atomic bomb.

Now, it is very amusing but this flippant approach is a historic approach to very serious problems which we have had from the Greeks on up and down the scale.

Barr: It is a perpetual generation gap.

Skolnick: I think there are differences in the generations. However, it hasn't grown up. I think this is the generation gap.

Jenner: I don't see that as anything other than an advocacy.

Barr: I had the impression from this very little experience with Hayden that I can talk to him and we are going to understand each other but we are going to have to make up our minds, we are going to have to talk probably in his language or mine—probably his—if we are going to talk.

I think he knows what I am thinking, and I think I know what he is thinking, but if we are going to talk about it, we are going to have to agree on a style of talking or we are not going to talk.

Harris: I am not sure he knows what you are thinking.

Barr: Well, what I represent to him he knows.

Harris: When Brown expresses the amazement of his generation and those younger people that concentrated work in the political forum will bring results, which is exactly what people have been saying to him, I wonder if we have been communicating with these people?

Skolnick: I wonder if I can go back to the symbolism business because I think it is kind of important. I think a lot of the actual violence is derived from symbolic forms of protest.

Now, I think the use of obscenity, which interestingly enough I think acts much to the disadvantage of the groups that are using it in terms of the larger political arena, is very important. It is important because it is a means of distinguishing themselves from their parents.

You see, those people are your children; in effect, this is what they are. Now, a guy who is starving, who is a worker and who is in revolution, he doesn't need to use symbolic means. Indeed, it is kind of interesting that is, recently, you see, that you find some black people using symbolic means. Olympic athletes.

These are guys who made it in the society and they want to distinguish themselves from the rest of the society and show a unity with another group, so they use a symbolic means and they evoke a response.

In Columbia, Chicago, I think the use of symbolism—of the anarchist flag, the Viet Cong flag, obscenity, and so forth —was the sort of thing that evoked an enormous response on the part of the police.

The police responded to the symbolism. So, I think this sort of symbolism is important in that the generation itself stresses it partly through obscenity, which is to show they are regular or something, and partly through a far more knowledgeable use and understanding of drugs than most adults have, and partly through wholly new music in a wholly new folk form so that Peter Seeger is an old man as far as they are concerned.

If you want to understand them, begin to listen to the lyrics of Bobby Dylan.

Horowitz: I think one other point must be raised with respect to the issue of dirty words and language. I don't think there is more obscenity in use now than in any other prior generation. I am told on good authority, for example, that President Johnson indulges in obscenity once in a while.

I think that the public and private use of obscenity is the key issue. For this generation the question of obscenity like the question of drugs is a matter of public privileges rather than private rights.

The transformation of what was a private matter into a public and demonstrably political matter is really significant in the anti-war protest movement of this generation.

Hoffer: Isn't it something in that fighting words have lost their bite. There used to be a time when you used these little words and had your teeth knocked in. And this is something to be alarmed about, when every word loses its bite. What happens to words is very important to society.

When I see fighting words lose their bite, I get alarmed.

Horowitz: Many things have lost their bite. It may be that certain forms of life, certain forms of sexuality have lost their bite, too. All kinds of things have lost their bite. I am not quite as alarmed over these things as Mr. Hoffer.

Somehow, it seems to me we have a perfect right to expect that for one generation what was private indulgence, for another generation may be viewed as a public act.

What we are witnessing now, if we are going to talk in

general terms, is a search for a higher morality. What young people are concerned with is the immoral basis of a private act. What was done formerly in the thirties and twenties as something surreptitious has now become publicly proper and the morality involved is the morality of full disclosure—of making things public.

This is where the anti-war movement and the question of violence is wrapped up in the larger question of generational hypocrisy and generational honesty.

Skolnick: That has been building up for a long time. I think in your generation ladies didn't smoke in public. I can recall my mother telling me, you know, that it was disgraceful for a lady to smoke in public. And some of you may be able to remember that, but even if you can't I hope you will take it as a fact that there was some reluctance on the part of ladies to smoke in public.

I think there have been many things made public which were formerly engaged in in private and were thought to be immoral. You can call it a loosening of morals if you want to disapprove of it, or you can call it a development of morality.

Barr: Maybe the rise of the female hemline is indicative of the whole problem.

Harris: But why do we use the term morality because I think we beg the question we were talking about—obscenity and cigarettes. Why don't we use the term taste which is what cigarette smoking becomes, what the use of certain letter configurations in fact becomes.

I think one of the errors we have made is to confuse these two terms. I think morality is something else. This is a taste question.

Skolnick: Well, one of the problems, I think we have attempted to use substantive criminal law as a way of solving social problems which were frequently taste problems.

For example, there is widespread use of marijuana in the colleges today. And yet this is a felony, you see.

Harris: That is not a taste problem, that goes to one's notion of health considerations, one's objective judgment about whether this is wise for the young or for anybody. But whether one uses certain configurations of letters which come out as Anglo-Saxon monosyllables, in my judgment is no longer then a taste question and until we see this we are going to have all kinds of problems.

Skolnick: Well, if you recall, the so-called filthy speech movement—which was not a movement at all—at the University of California came about as a result of the arrest of a young man who held up a sign that had a four-letter word on it.

So it wasn't simply a taste question; it was a question of community enforcing morality. Let's put it this way—that is the community's definition, because the man was arrested, so it couldn't have been simply a matter of taste.

Jaworski: I want to get back to one thing that interested me very much and that relates to the distinctions that you draw in acts of violence, particularly when you point out that some of these acts that have been discussed and perhaps one or two others were not motivated by any desirable personal gain. They are acts of violence that relate to doing it for the sake of a cause and so on.

To me the important thing is that it is a violation of the law. That is what it leads to. Frankly, I just don't see, from my standpoint, a whole lot to be gained by trying to excuse it on the ground that it isn't personal gain.

If I don't like, for instance, the loudness of the radio that my neighbor plays and I call him out and bust him in the nose, I have committed a crime. I have engaged in an act of lawlessness yet I didn't do it for any personal gain.

It didn't mean a darn to me. It gets back to all of these things as law violations. And they should be regarded as such. I am wondering if you don't agree?

Skolnick: Well, I have two responses. One is that from the point of view of doing an analysis of the causes of these actions it is simply analytically important to distinguish them. That really has nothing to do with whether I approve of them or not.

The second is that there are certain kinds of behavior in society that I think are generally regarded as reprehensible, murder, theft and so forth. There is a peripheral area of behavior that is controversial as to whether it is reprehensible or not. I think that is a fact.

It doesn't matter which side you come out on, but the fact is that certain behavior is controversial.

I will give you a famous example in criminal law—the Wolfson Report on whether homosexuality should be a crime. You can say, well, it is a violation of the law, but I submit to you from the point of view of sociologists examining this phenomenon it makes a difference as to whether the population against whom the laws are being enforced accepts the justification for the law.

Jaworski: This is where we get into dangerous areas, I think. Because you and I may be in agreement on what is a reprehensible act and we may find another group that has an entirely different view on it.

Skolnick: But if we want to understand the causes and prevention of violence, I am purposely moving away from that, but if we want to understand the causes and preventions of any kind of social phenomena, I would say the causes—like saying we are going to have laws against homosexuality no matter what happens, that is a matter of judgment.

Jaworski: Well, as far as I am concerned, as long as you have the law, the law should be enforced, and I think it is well for us to know the motivation. I think that is very important.

Higginbotham: Well, I think we have a presentation problem, very candidly. I would be absolutely delighted, as I was to hear from you this morning, and am absolutely delighted to hear from Professor Horowitz, but I want for Professor Horowitz to interpret his view and you to interpret yours. Now, I am totally confused as to whether you are speaking for Professor Horowitz. I think from a presentation standpoint we should have one person present this and then for you to comment on it afterwards, and then I think we will get shared reactions to the matters at hand.

Menninger: May I say that my impression is that we are getting a sociological analysis of the anti-war movement which we have heard various aspects of today and then we are having some discussion on this. Am I correct in my assumption?

Skolnick: Yes, and we are really giving you our present thoughts which are not necessarily our final thoughts but our analysis of the testimony heard today in the light of the research that Professor Horowitz has done. And I think I had better keep quiet and let him finish.

Horowitz: Mr. Jaworski, you are raising a very major consideration. One point that I would raise is the possibility of obsolescence of law. We ought not to overlook the one vital aspect of law that is usually unspoken: namely that laws often are never fully executed or acted upon.

The whole world of marriage and divorce laws is a good indication of an area in which normal patterns of behavior supersede certain statutory codes.

There are all kinds of confusions in the legal system that are never really resolved at the level of the law. On the other hand, one does not really await legal resolution, but simply responds to normative patterns.

One very vital area of concern of the Commission is precisely another fresh look at the connection of law and violence. This whole area of how the legal definition of violence might have to be altered so that we develop a more omnibus approach to questions not necessarily of violence but distinguishing violence, civil disobedience or violence of property versus crimes against persons. Distinctions of this type may well turn out to be some of the more important findings worked on by the Commission.

To get back to the last point, while the anti-war movement often simulates many tactics of the black liberation movement, the former is clearly concerned with a response to the alienation of the affluent youth, whereas the latter is concerned with problems of wider participation in the benefits of the American society.

At this point we can sharply distinguish the black and white forms of left-wing participation in American society. From here we may wish to distinguish attitudes on the part of the white community toward black and white forms of protest.

I believe strongly that there is perhaps a much greater degree of resentment to white forms of protest among certain sectors of American society, since the black forms of protest are really a part of American dreams of greater participation through existing channels.

Higginbotham: By whom?

Horowitz: On the part of many people involved in decision-making. Even the white working class might have more resentment ultimately for white forms of protest than black forms of protest, not because white workers necessarily appreciate or hope for Negro liberation, but because it is generally a question of involvement and participation rather than a response to hard-to-appreciate alienation and separation.

Harris: Don't you have to distinguish here when you said establishment, I said all right, you carved out a group. When you were talking about leadership, dislike of a movement, I might agree with you.

When you talk about mass reaction, lower middle-class and lower-class reaction, unless you really meant to put that word in there, I couldn't disagree with you more. The undercurrent of the Wallace movement is an anti-black movement which is buttressed by the anti-student movement but in the absence of the fear of the black, I doubt that it could exist.

Horowitz: The distinction you make between the elite and the rank and file masses is very important.

I wouldn't want to disparage that difference one iota. I prefaced my remark that in this instance I was moving in an area of hunch. I do believe that among the elite as well as the mass there might be more resentment for the white middle class anti-war movement than there would be for the Negro liberation movement. As we move down the scale of power, there might be a reversal of that phenomena and that would certainly be worth going into much further. My point is simply that the working classes are raising Hobbesian rather than Marxian demands—for social order rather than justice.

Harris: But it is much more important in terms of society and consequence and it is not the kind of difference that you know in passion but it is a difference of such degree that it becomes a difference in kind.

Horowitz: I am inclined to agree with you wholeheartedly. We have to analyze where the cut-off point is. Let's put it that way. It is an empirical problem and it will take much homework to solve it.

The final point is again highlighted from other testimony heard today that the current movement against the war is characterized by a fractionalism that is a consequence of the fragmentation of the anti-war movement, into specifically anti-Vietnam protest, others to the anti-draft movement, others linked to the anti-American posture and others to a general religious opposition to war in general.

Each of these areas are potentially volatile for precisely the reason that there is an absence of organizational restraint or definition of clear goals. There is a kind of paradox. On one hand the anti-war movement is in such a thirst for elemental participation in the American society that some of the more intimate forms of representational democracy get bypassed and downgraded.

This related back to the first point in my presentation. Since there exist nuclear kinds of groupings with very low level organization interaction, the spontaneous factor becomes much higher. Since the acceptance of orthodox definitions of democracy would downgrade the theory of spontaneous behavior and generation of politics we hear little of the democratic aspirations in the anti-war movement. This completes the organizational aspects of my testimony, and hopefully we can move into other areas not covered in my formal analysis.

Higginbotham: Thank you. Do any of my colleagues have any questions?

Harris: I have one. We often look for solutions which are dim and unclear and ignore potential relationships that would occur to the average mind.

The thing that interests me about the student movement throughout the world is that—even though I reject the approach—all of them follow the revisionism of the Red Guards in China.

I mentioned at lunch the fact that Mao is an old anarchist and perhaps, as suggested by an old friend of mine, an unreconstructed anarchist.

I wonder if you have done anything in the way of analyzing not in old-fashioned Comintern relationships? That is, those of us who have relationships with old-fashioned ways in which international movements get promoted and whether you have looked at the possibility of an influence of significance of first of all a kind of Maoist dislike of any kind of organization which is continual and the exemplary function of the Red Guard revisionism which took place in China?

I keep having the feeling that the similarity is not coincidental without suggesting the kind of Comintern relationship that was the experience of the twenties and thirties.

Skolnick: I would think you could find far more similarity if you were to read Henry David Thoreau's essay on civil disobedience. The kind of moralism is so rooted in the whole New England movement, I think it is much closer than Mao.

Of course, there are a number of cultural features that you can find in all of these groups, but I think this sort of influence is probably far greater than Mao's influence even though there is a mouthing of Mao.

Because of the situation in this country, I think, the affluence and so forth lends itself much more to the idea of the guy who is going to spend the night in jail and set an example for his neighbors, that sort of thing.

Harris: Well, our culture is not irrelevant but is it explanatory? Because then you have to say, and Germany and France and Mexico, and, and, and.

I simply raise the question because I have seen inadequate evidence of this possibility of the relationship.

Horowitz: Ambassador Harris raises a perfectly reasonable question and one that I agree with. I think it is much more important to familiarize ourselves at the moment with Mao Tse-tung than Henry David Thoreau. I wrote an article with a colleague in the November of 1966 issue of *Trans-action* on the Red Guard phenomena. There are very powerful similarities with our own anti-war protest movement. Mao does represent that generation that made the revolution and he has the qualities of leadership that impress the young. How do you prevent the revolution from being corrupted? How do you prevent happening in China what took place in the Soviet Union? These key problems of the revolutionary generation in China were solved by passing up the middle generation in favor of the youthful generation. The anti-bureaucratic ethic does get taken up in organizational form. I agree wholeheartedly with you that the attitude of the Red Guard toward organization is an important aspect in the current movement and it ought to be more closely examined.

Harris: I hope you will because I think we may make a contribution here, because nobody else is really doing it.

Horowitz: May I suggest you look at the new book by Robert Jay Lifton entitled *Revolutionary Immortality,* on this very subject, a brilliant book.

Higginbotham: Do you have any comment as to anything which was said today, or any of the questions which have been presented to any of your colleagues?

Horowitz: No, I have none.

Jenner: I am interested in the papers submitted which you summarized as your conclusions, to say the choice is either a democratic society or a garrison state. The question you pose is the price Americans are willing to pay for law and order, the elimination of crime in the streets, that concept of it, and whether or not this price might be far more pervasive and pernicious than that being paid for the present levels of violence. Is it your current judgment, Mr. Skolnick, that the democratic society to which we adhere and which has brought us where we are, good or bad or indifferent, necessarily carries with it, as part of freedom of dissent, freedom of speech, the exercise of some additional rights, necessarily carries with it somewhat violence, and if you substitute for that society a law and order society, as you say, the garrison state, the Hitler character of society, which didn't last very long, fortunately, then you destroy these other values which are really the values that the people want when they sit down and think about it?

Horowitz: Clearly, Mr. Jenner, you raise one of the most important possible questions that I know of. All sociological literature points to the fact, when there is high social mobility, there obtains high social deviance. When there is rapid mobility in the industrial sector, society has to pay a price for such change in terms of disorganization and deviant patterns of behavior, especially among the young. One definition of development itself—industrial, political and economic— involved breaking norms, breaking established patterns, engaging in certain forms of deviance that may involve the spillovers into violent forms of action.

The question of deviance, violence, and social change is an empirical one. It cannot be a categorical one. If you attempt a categorical response in your final summary report, then it seems to me that the very purpose of the Commission itself may be seriously questioned. Because what you are engaged in, as increasingly must become evident, is the empirical sources that are powerful in stimulating a violent response to social unrest. That seems to me to be a form that we all have to operate in. We may disagree violently over the amount of violence tolerable or permissible. But when a man declares that in his society there is no violence, you may also be sure he is saying in his society there is no development, no social change, and no democracy.

Therefore, in some sense it would be worse to make the assumption that an absence of violence is a guarantee of utopia than that the presence of violence is consonant with democracy. I don't think we ought to be guilty of that kind of absolutistic, moralistic formulation. The better part of wisdom is to recognize that much of what we are doing today in describing violence is in the nature of politics.

Mr. Hoffer said to one of the earlier witnesses, that what

he really wants is political participation, but he is not ready for it. The answer should have been, at least the answer I would give, is that political participation is precisely what the anti-war movement is after.

Jenner: That is what I thought the witness was going to say, but he didn't.

Higginbotham: He should have said yes, and we are as ready as others have been.

Professor Skolnick, I want you free to join in the dialogue. My colleagues sort of implied to me that we had been adjourning at 5:00, but I have as much seat power as they.

Jenner: May I say to the Chairman, if you are intimidated, it is the first time in your life that you have been.

Menninger: I have listened with a different kind of concern, partly because of my focus on individual factors, but also on the question of—well, your formulation that if you have democracy, violence is inevitable; that is part of what you are saying. My rationale as to why violence may be inevitable might start in different areas. The question is what kind of devices can we develop, whatever be the rationale for the origin of violence, what kind of rationale can we develop to more effectively deal with it?

The guidelines offered by President Brewster were remarkable, but he also made a notation of failure in executive and legislative leadership. What kind of escape valves can we develop? How do we develop ways to encourage respect for individuals and enhance the communications process?

I hope these are some of the things that you are addressing. I must confess that I enjoy your editorials in *Transaction* and I have great expectations for its future growth.

Horowitz: I am going to waive on that question for one obvious reason; it is very late. Further, many of my colleagues are going to be dealing with that. I know Mr. Skolnick has been sitting up half the night on precisely that question and to-morrow or the day after those issues will be addressed. I will use the coward's way out and not reply by saying my professional brethren will answer those questions.

Jenner: Well, as we leave, could I observe to Professor Horowitz and Professor Skolnick, getting back to the question of taste and the question of ladies smoking in public, my mother believes that ladies should not smoke at all, but she had trouble with that concept in presenting it to my sister, due to the fact that my grandmother, her mother, smokes a clay pipe.

Barr: Let me just identify this memorandum that was circulated to you. This is the memorandum that Tom Hayden identified in his testimony that purports to come from the files of the Selective Service. It is very interesting and I suggest you might want to read it overnight.

Jenner: The memorandum that Mr. Hayden referred to?

Barr: Yes. You have in front of you one of the memoranda prepared by the Selective Service System that he identified in the course of his testimony.

Menninger: I would hope we wouldn't have to wait until reading it to ascertain whether or not it is a legitimate document.

Barr: Well, that isn't always an easy process.

Higginbotham: We want to thank you, Dr. Horowitz, for your presentation. We stand adjourned.

[Whereupon, at 5:25 P.M., the commission was recessed, to reconvene at 10:00 A.M. Thursday, 23 October, 1968.]

EPILOGUE: 1970

Two years have passed since the completion of the main body of the text for *The Struggle Is the Message*. Though the war in Vietnam and the protest against that war continue, certain critical changes have taken place, both in the political structure of the American nation and in the political attitudes of the American people.

The shift from Johnson to Nixon meant (1) the "Vietnamization" and gradual de-escalation of the Vietnam conflict; (2) the continued belief in the Cold War ideology that produced our involvement in the first place, as is shown by the increasing commitment to the protection of anti-Communist leaders in Southeast Asian countries such as Laos and Cambodia; and (3) an attempt to co-opt the symbols of peace by seeking a broad accommodation with the Soviet Union along the lines of a Metternichian settlement and by delegitimizing protest. The Nixon administration has been able to do these three things with considerable success because of the traditional isolationism of the Republican Party at least as much as the political acumen of the present administration. Not incidentally, the decline in governmental war fervor is clearly linked to the high domestic costs of international violence; to the pressure to satisfy immediate needs of minority and ethnic groups within the United States, even if this means a reduction of priorities for the overseas military operation. The American black people, although more separated from the peace movement in 1970 than ever before, ironically serve that peace movement more profoundly than any direct form of struggle precisely because of widespread insistence on a reordering of national priorities that places domestic tranquillity above international conflict.

Meanwhile, the anti-war movement has responded to the gradually cooling war fever in several major, and not necessarily compatible, ways. Pro-peace Democrats have been able, by their being part of the party out of power, to work more openly for peace. The Kennedy and McCarthy supporters in particular have joined the New Democratic Coalition in the "Marches on Washington" and "Days of Moratorium" held on October, November, and April 15. But these forms of anti-war protest, although still generating large numbers of supporters, have not materially affected the conduct or outcome of the war. Indeed, many of the Democratic leaders protesting the war are handicapped by being associated with the political party largely responsible for the extensive military involvement in Vietnam. They are hardly in a position to attack the Republican administration for waging war.

The inability of either major party to mount and sustain a meaningful peace offensive has led to "politics of the body," or as I call it in the text, "pragmatic violence." This politics emphasizes the practicality of attacking a convenient symbol of the enemy rather than trying to change the conventional political pattern. It is easier to attack Dow Chemical Company recruiting agents or the ROTC facilities at major campuses than to confront the abstract political basis of the war. The deeds of the anti-war movement remain very much within a symbolic and pragmatic context, although protesters have grown increasingly strident and desperate during the past several years.

In fact, the demand for revolution has superseded the demand for peace among the radicals of the "peace forces." For them, the war in Vietnam is only a symptom of the imperialist malaise in American society. Therefore they focus attention on the imperialist core of America rather than the military limits of the war. This change in the evaluation of the conflict in American society characterizes the present period. The anti-war radicals of 1964-1968 have become the anti-imperialist radicals of 1970. Along with this change in ideology has come a change in tactics. Today's radicals dismiss nonviolent methods as impractical, a judgment partially formed by the assassination of Robert Kennedy and Martin Luther King.

In this context, the Conspiracy Trials in Chicago, and trials scheduled for the Weatherman faction of the SDS and for many portions of the Black Panther Party, reveal the polarization of American society: pro-government forces calling for "law and order" oppose anti-government forces advocating total revolution. Just as the harassing of voter registration campaigns in the South stimulated black militancy, the persecution of the anti-war movement made dissenters into radicals and then into revolutionaries. The politics of simplification characteristic of the sixties have now given way to the politics of oversimplification. Today's polarities of reaction and revolution have a classic, clean look that the anti-war movement could never boast, for the anti-war movement always assumed that it was within the established tradition of protest. The "dialogues" took place not only within the anti-war movement but with leading figures of the Establishment. But revolutionists must deny the viability or legitimacy of the established government; and conversely, the government must deny the legitimacy of claims made by the revolutionists. The Establishment considers the present revolutionists as less anti-war than pro-Viet Cong, as internal enemies instead of pacifist dissenters. Indeed, the militants cheering for a Viet Cong victory emphasize a clearcut struggle between reaction and revolution, rather than a reasoning together toward consensus.

The much heralded "silent majority" still remains largely silent and largely leaderless, at least in national politics. The president commands a large following not on the basis of his international politics, but simply as the titular national leader. As the politics of protest have been transformed into the politics of polarization, the silent majority has been less, rather than more, decisive in settling the national malaise over the war question. In fact, the American public has now been able to live with the idea of war for the three decades since the beginning of World War II. If the silent American has a marked distaste for war as a national issue, he has shown a rare ability to accommodate himself to war as a national style. Thus insofar as masses must support political policies, the American masses continue to underwrite war. It is not so much that they consciously wish to pursue any specific conflict or that they have a pathological fear of world Communism (although that element remains in existence). It is rather that Americans have come to accept warfare as a permanent feature of the economy and the polity—and as a result they remain unpersuaded by either pacifist or militant protest. The "prosperity" of recent years serves to reinforce the popular belief that war is good for the economy and therefore good for the country.

It is conceivable that with the ideological divisions between generations, and the intensification of racial separatism, a coming together of disaffected numbers of the American people will serve warning that the war system—however viable it may seem at the economic level—is no longer tolerable as a national political style. And in this connection it may be that just as violence is the outcome of political struggles, so too the anti-war movement may be the prelude to wider rumblings in the bowels of the American federalist system. At any rate it now seems certain that the anti-war movement has lost much of its autonomy. Its organization and ideology are being subsumed into more directly political struggles: party conflicts within the liberal faction and revolutionary violence within the radical faction. These two factions may soon lock horns in mortal combat, which indicates how far we have come in a few short years from the halcyon days of the teach-ins and the be-ins. How that struggle, or the recent struggles of the anti-war movement as a whole, will change American society is still in doubt. But the dissenters have raised issues that will not be settled easily or quickly.

APPENDIX

FOUR TABLES ON
ANTI-WAR DEMONSTRATIONS

Like most tables, these four oversimplify reality. The financial and human resources at my disposal in the compilation of these materials were restricted; more time and money would have allowed me to explore more fully the size and scope of the anti-war movement (particularly the demonstrations by fewer than 1,000 persons). The information came from secondary sources, which are necessarily limited and fragmentary. The basic ones were the *New York Times, Newsweek* (including its research library facilities), *Facts on File,* and the *Riot Data Review* (issued by the Lemberg Center for the Study of Violence at Brandeis University).

The most serious drawback in these tables is the problem of spillover mentioned in chapter one. A rally or riot with the goal of bridging the gap between black liberation and anti-war movements, or changing the university administration through an anti-war issue, raises a serious problem of classification.

Because of the difficulty in isolating violence in the anti-war movement from urban or ghetto violence, I have included in these tables only those rallies and riots with a *stated* anti-war purpose. If the anti-war aspect was one of several items in the list of grievances, the marches are listed; if not—even if the majority of demonstrators were white college students—the item is not listed. The tabular materials, imperfect as they are, reinforce the claim that the struggle, rather than any specific grievance, is the message.

I.L.H.

147

TABLE I: ANTI-WAR DEMONSTRATIONS BY 1000 OR MORE PERSONS

DATE	PLACE	SIZE	ORGANIZATIONAL SPONSORSHIP	TACTICS
1965: March 12	White House, Washington, D.C.	15,000	Students for a Democratic Society (SDS), Women Strike for Peace (WSP), Student Nonviolent Coordinating Committee (SNCC)	Picket, then march to Washington Monument for rally
June 8	Madison Square Garden, NYC	17,000	Committee for a Sane Nuclear Policy (SANE)	Rally (indoors)
June 8	UN Headquarters, NYC	2,000	SANE	March from Madison Square Garden to UN
August 6	White House	1,000	Committee for Nonviolent Action (CNVA), War Resisters' League, Catholic Workers	Picket and sit-in for Hiroshima anniversary
October 15	Nationwide	70,000– 100,000	National Coordinating Committee to End the War in Vietnam	Rally, march, picket
October 15	Berkeley, Calif.	10,000	Vietnam Day Committee	March to Oakland Army Base (halted at city limits)
October 16	New York City	10,000– 14,000	Committee for a Fifth Avenue Peace Parade	March down Fifth Avenue
October 16	Berkeley	3,000	Vietnam Day Committee	March to Oakland Army Base (stopped)
October 16	Civic Center, San Francisco	2,000	unreported	Rally
October 16	Boston	2,000	unreported	Demonstrate on Common
November 6	Union Square, NYC	1,500	CNVA	Rally (5 burn draft cards)
November 20	Berkeley	8,000	Vietnam Day Committee	March to Oakland Park

Date	Location	Number	Organization	Action
November 27	Washington, D.C.	15,000-35,000	SANE	March
1966:				
February 9	Washington, D.C.	1,500	WSP	Picket White House and Congressional offices
February 20	Town Hall, NYC	1,500	Committee of the Professions to End the War in Vietnam	"Read-in" for peace
February 23	Madison Square Garden, NYC	4,000	unreported	Picket speech by President Johnson
March 2	Cobo Hall, Detroit	1,000	unreported	Demonstrate
March 25-27	Worldwide	50,000	National Coordinating Committee	Rally, walk-in, sit-in, picket, march for International Days of Protest
March 26	San Francisco	3,500	unreported	March to Civic Center for rally (black armbands and cardboard coffins)
March 26	Coliseum, Chicago	2,000	unreported	Rally (Staughton Lynd and Julian Bond speak)
March 26	New York City	20,000-25,000	Fifth Avenue Peace Parade Committee	Parade down Fifth Avenue; rally at Mall (A. J. Muste, Norman Mailer, Donald Duncan speak)
April 16	Times Square, NYC	4,500	Fifth Avenue Peace Parade Committee, WSP (separate vigil)	March
May 15	Washington, D.C.	8,000-11,000	SANE	Picket White House; rally at Washington Monument in support of peace candidates

TABLE I—Continued

DATE	PLACE	SIZE	ORGANIZATIONAL SPONSORSHIP	TACTICS
(1966)				
May 18	Madison, Wisc.	10,000	unreported	Hold anti-draft rally supporting administration building takeover (following Chicago takeover on draft rankings and deferment tests)
August 6	Times Square	5,000	Fifth Avenue Peace Parade Committee, National Coordinating Committee to End the War in Vietnam	Rally for Hiroshima anniversary, picket Dow Chemical Co.; hold vigil at UN
August 6	Independence Hall, Philadelphia	1,000	National Coordinating Committee	Rally
August 6	San Francisco	4,000	National Coordinating Committee	Parade
December 1	U. of Calif., Berkeley	5,000	unreported	Boycott classes after police break up protest of Navy recruiting table
1967:				
January 31	White House	2,000	Concerned Clergy	March to demand bombing halt
February 15	Pentagon, Washington, D.C.	2,500	WSP	Women picket and storm building
March 25	Chicago	5,000	Southern Christian Leadership Conference (SCLC)	SCLC and M. L. King march to Coliseum
April 15	New York City	100,000-125,000	Spring Mobilization to End the War in Vietnam (headed by Rev. Bevel of SCLC)	March from Central Park to UN (speeches by M. L. King, Benjamin Spock and Stokely Carmichael; 200 burn draft cards)
April 15	San Francisco	50,000	Spring Mobilization and Black Nationalists	March to and rally at Kezar Stadium (Julian Bond, Mrs. M. L. King, Robert Scheer speak)
October 17	Oakland, Calif.	3,000	Stop the Draft Steering Committee, SDS, New Politics, SNCC	Bar entrance at Induction Center

Date	Location	Number	Organization	Action
October 18	U. of Wisc., Madison	1,000	unreported	Riot against Dow
October 19	Brooklyn	1,000	unreported	Sit-in at school building to protest Navy recruitment
October 20	Brooklyn	8,000	unreported	Boycott school, protest police brutality
October 20	Induction Center, Oakland	6,500	Stop the Draft Steering Committee, SDS, New Politics, SNCC	Hold silent vigil (cars, signs, trash cans block traffic)
October 21-22	Pentagon	55,000-150,000	National Mobilization Committee to End the War in Vietnam	Seek confrontation; rally and storm Pentagon, sit-in, and hold silent vigils
October 21	Madison	1,800	unreported	Protest use of State Capitol by city police suppressing anti-draft demonstrations on university campus
November 14	Hilton Hotel, NYC	3,000	Fifth Avenue Peace Parade Committee, SDS	Picket speech by Dean Rusk; demonstrate on all levels
November 20	San Jose, Calif.	2,000	unreported	Demonstrate against Dow
December 4-8	Whitehall Induction Center, NYC	25,000	unreported	Attempt to close down the center (Stop the Draft Week)
1968:				
January 29	New York City	1,000	unreported	Rally for Spock
April 23	Columbia U., NYC	10,000	SDS, Black Student Union and other campus-based political groups	Prevent gymnasium construction encroaching upon Harlem property; halt contract work by Columbia with Institute of Defense Analysis (IDA)

TABLE I—Continued

DATE (1968)	PLACE	SIZE	ORGANIZATIONAL SPONSORSHIP	TACTICS
April 23	Oakland	2,000	unidentified	Demonstrate (hoping to bridge the gap between the anti-war movement and the black liberation movement)
April 26	800 campuses	200,000	Student Mobilization Committee	Strike classes
April 27	New York City	87,000-100,000	National Mobilization Committee Coalition for an Anti-Imperialist March (Youth Against War and Fascism pull out because Mayor Lindsay speaks; 400 hold own and most violent rally)	Rally in Central Park for N.Y. Loyalty Day: Mrs. King, Lindsay speak (Youth Against War and the National Liberation Front show up in helmets for own rally)
August 28	Chicago	9,000-14,000	National Mobilization Committee (including SCLC, SDS, Youth International Party and other militant groups)	Joint rallies of 35 anti-war organizations at Democratic Party Nominating Convention hotel headquarters; attempted marches to convention site.

TABLE II: ANTI-WAR DEMONSTRATIONS BY FEWER THAN 1000 PERSONS

DATE 1965:	PLACE	SIZE	ORGANIZATIONAL SPONSORSHIP	TACTICS
February 19	New York City	14	CNVA	Picket US-UN mission (intent to arrest announced)
February 20	New York City	19	CNVA	Picket Peace on Earth Conference
February 20	White House	400	CNVA	Picket
April 20	White House	17	unreported	Sit-in
May 7	Columbia U.	200	unreported	Rally
May 12	Pentagon	500-1,000	Clergymen plus various groups	Hold silent vigil

Date	Location	Number	Sponsor	Activity
May 15	New York City	250	N.Y. Workshop in Nonviolence, SDS, WRL, Catholic Workers, Student Peace Union	Countermarch on Armed Forces Day; 29 sit-in
May 15	Times Square	300	Youth Against War in Vietnam	Rally
June 16	Pentagon	200	CNVA	Roam corridors, hand out pamphlets
August 6	Oakland	200	Vietnam Day Committee	Try to stop troop train
August 8	White House	36	Assembly of Unrepresented People	Try to block entrance
August 9	Capitol, Washington, D.C.	800	Assembly of Unrepresented People	March on Capitol from Washington Monument
August 12	Oakland	300	Vietnam Day Committee	Attempt to halt troop train (some board train)
August 23	Oakland	60	Vietnam Day Committee	Attempt to halt troop train (leap from tracks at last minute as train never slowed down)
October 15	Selective Service Office, Ann Arbor, Mich.	n.a.	National Coordinating Committee	Lie-in
October 15	Madison	300	unreported	Rally
October 15	Boston	750	unreported	Rally
October 15	Wayne State U., Detroit	400	unreported	Teach-in
October 15	U. of Calif., Santa Barbara	300	unreported	Rally
October 15	U. of Colo., Boulder	100	unreported	Rally

TABLE II—Continued

DATE (1965)	PLACE	SIZE	ORGANIZATIONAL SPONSORSHIP	TACTICS
October 15	Chicago	200	unreported	Demonstrate
October 15	Buffalo, N.Y.	80	National Coordinating Committee	Demonstrate
October 15	Iowa State U., Ames	12	unreported	Picket U.S. Navy Reserve
October 15	Yale U., New Haven, Conn.	250	unreported	Rally
October 15	City College of New York, NYC	600	unreported	Rally and hold vigil
October 15	Whitehall Induction Center, NYC	400	SDS, WRL, Committee for Nonviolent Action, Youth Against War and Fascism	Rally (David Miller burns draft card)
October 15	Columbus, Ohio	n.a.	unreported	Rally (aborted when march leaders arrested)
October 16	Baltimore, Md.	60	unreported	Picket speech by Rusk
October 16	Austin, Texas	120	National Coordinating Committee	Picket
October 16	Chicago	150	unreported	Picket
October 16	State Capitol, Salem, Ore.	400	unreported	Picket
October 16	Carbondale, Ill.	70	unreported	Picket
October 16	Williams College, Williamstown, Mass.	50	unreported	March from Bennington to Williams
October 16	Philadelphia	350	National Coordinating Committee	March from City Hall to U. of Penna.

Date	Location	Number	Group	Action
October 16	Federal Building, Trenton, N.J.	400	unreported	Picket
October 16	Ann Arbor	400	unreported	Picket jail demanding release of demonstrators held for October 15 lie-in
October 16	Truax AFB, Madison	40	unreported	Try to make citizens' arrest of base commander
October 16	Cornell U., Ithaca, N.Y.	300	unreported	Hold silent vigil after Homecoming game
October 28	Washington U., St. Louis	40	SDS	Picket Vice Pres. Humphrey
November 2	Pentagon	1	individual	Norman Morrison immolates self
November 9	UN Headquarters	1	individual	Roger LaPorte immolates self
November 11	South Bend, Ind.	1	individual	Woman attempts immolation
December 4	Chancery, NYC	50	Fordham University students	Protest Berrigan banishment
1966:				
February 3	Philadelphia	175	Bryn Mawr, Swarthmore, Haverford students	Fast (8 days)
February 5	Washington, D.C.	100	unreported	Veterans turn in discharge papers
February 5	New York City	750	Fifth Avenue Peace Parade Committee	Picket US-UN mission
February 12	New York City	800	Ad Hoc Committee to Support the February 12 Demonstrations	March through midtown (rally at St. Mark's in the Bouwerie)
February 26	White House	100	Poverty Workers for Peace	Picket
March 12	Union Square	125	Student Peace Union	Rally

TABLE II—Continued

DATE (1966)	PLACE	SIZE	ORGANIZATIONAL SPONSORSHIP	TACTICS
March 24	New York City	3	CNVA	Destroy draft cards in front of TV cameras
March 25	Union Square	300	Veterans and Reservists to End the War in Vietnam	Rally (15 burn discharge papers)
March 25	Ann Arbor	200	National Coordinating Committee	Walk-in at draft boards
March 25	Selective Service Testing Center, Chicago	9	National Coordinating Committee	Sit-in
March 25	Boston Army Base	n.a.	National Coordinating Committee	Picket
March 26	White House	200	National Coordinating Committee	Picket
March 26	Boston	700	SDS, CNVA	March from Cambridge to Arlington St. Church
March 26	Philadelphia	700	National Coordinating Committee	March to Independence Hall
March 31	Courthouse, Boston	11	National Coordinating Committee	Demonstrate on steps (2 burn draft cards)
April 1	Boston	60	unreported	Hold vigils for those jailed
April 6	Boston	300	unreported	March to protest lack of police protection for demonstrators
April 10	New York City	190	Veterans and Reservists, N.Y. Workshop for Nonviolent Action	March up Fifth Avenue; mill-in at Easter Parade
April 12	Stock Exchange, NYC	11	Youth Against War and Fascism	Disrupt trading
April 14	New York City	75	Youth Against War and Fascism	Protest in financial district

Date	Location	Number	Organization	Action
April 23	Portsmouth, N.H.	50	American Friends Service Committee	March to naval base
May 7	New York City	400	Ad Hoc Committee for the Women's Peace March	Rally at midtown shopping center
May 12	Chicago	350	SDS, National Coordinating Committee	Sit-in against draft ranking
May 13	City College of New York	150	unreported	Sit-in against draft deferment test
May 19	Brooklyn College, NYC	75	unreported	Sit-in against draft
May 19	Roosevelt U., Chicago	n.a.	unreported	Sit-in against draft
May 21	New York City	300	Workshop in Nonviolent Action	Disrupt Armed Forces Day Parade by sit-in
May 24	Hunter College, NYC	n.a.	unreported	Demonstrate against draft
June 29	New York City	700	Workshop, Committee for Nonviolent Action, W.E.B. DuBois Club, WSP	Picket US-UN mission after bombing near Hanoi
July 1	New York City	n.a.	Workshop for Nonviolent Action	Picket US-UN mission after bombing of Hanoi
July 4	Independence Hall	400	CNVA	Picket George Ball
July 21	Groton, Conn.	150	CNVA	Picket launching of Polaris sub
August 6	Madison	n.a.	unreported	Hold vigil at ROTC building
August 6	Washington, D.C.	n.a.	SNCC	Picket National Shrine and Luci Johnson's wedding
August 9	New York City	200	unreported	Picket Dow on Nagasaki anniversary

TABLE II—Continued

DATE (1966)	PLACE	SIZE	ORGANIZATIONAL SPONSORSHIP	TACTICS
August 17-18	12th Army Headquarters, Atlanta	20	SNCC	Demonstrate (ejected from Center)
November 7	Harvard U., Cambridge, Mass.	100	SDS	Shout down Robert McNamara
November 15	Brown U., Providence, R.I.	100	unreported	Protest General Wheeler's speech
1967:				
January 17	St. Patrick's Cathedral, NYC	75	Catholic Peace Fellowship	Protest Cardinal Spellman's Vietnam position
January 22	St. Patrick's Cathedral	23	unreported	Disrupt High Mass
January 22	Madison	100	SDS	Protest Dow recruiter
February 13	Harvard U.	500	SDS	March against Arthur Goldberg
March 8	New York City	50	unreported	Walk out of National Book Awards (addressed by Humphrey)
March 31	Selective Service headquarters, Washington, D.C.	18	unreported	Picket (David Miller sits down wanting arrest)
April 24	Austin	100	SDS	Jeer Humphrey speech to Texas Legislature
May 8	House Office Bldg., Washington, D.C.	50	unreported	Protest draft
May 10	Pentagon	18	unreported	Hold vigil outside Joint Chiefs of Staff offices

Date	Location	Number	Organization	Action
May 17	White House	200	Spring Mobilization Committee	Demonstrate and demand to see President (led by Spock)
May 29	Treasury Building, Washington, D.C.	30	American Friends Service Committee	Wait-in (bank accounts for North Vietnamese wounded frozen by government)
September 20	White House	500	WSP	Picket (permit allows 100 to picket; fight)
October 8	Williams College	75	unreported	Walk out of Mrs. Johnson's speech
October 9	Yale U.	750	unreported	Hold silent vigil while Mrs. Johnson talks
October 16	Federal Building, Los Angeles	300	The Resistance	Rally on steps (8 destroy draft cards)
October 16	Federal Building, Chicago	140	Chicago Area Draft Resistance (CADRE)	Picket (5 enter, refuse to leave)
October 16	Boston	280	unreported	Burn draft cards or give them to clergy of Arlington St. Church
October 16	Independence Hall	175	unreported	Demonstrate (5 burn cards)
October 16	Induction Center, Cincinnati	150	unreported	March
October 16	Ithaca	200	unreported	March to Selective Service headquarters (15 turn in cards)
October 16	Federal Courthouse, NYC	300	unreported	Turn in draft cards (barred from entering)
October 16	Induction Center Oakland	500	Stop the Draft Steering Committee, New Politics, SDS, SNCC	Picket, sit-in to bar entrance

TABLE II—Continued

DATE (1967)	PLACE	SIZE	ORGANIZATIONAL SPONSORSHIP	TACTICS
October 19	Induction Center, Chicago	100	CADRE, SDS	Try to break in
October 20	Columbia U.	330	SDS	Demand end to CIA recruiting and IDA support
October 23	Princeton U., Princeton, N.J.	50	SDS	Sit-in at IDA building (30 refuse to leave)
October 24	U. of Minn., Minneapolis	20	unreported	Sleep-in against Dow at administration building
October 25	U. of Ill., Urbana	300	unreported	Picket Dow recruitment
October 25	Harvard U.	200	unreported	Sit-in at Dow room; hold recruiter prisoner
October 25	Detroit	700	unreported	Demonstrate (Concerned Clergy announce they will aid and abet draft resisters)
October 26	Oberlin College, Oberlin, Ohio	100	unreported	Surround car of Navy recruiters
October 27	Selective Service headquarters, Baltimore	3	Baltimore Interfaith Mission	Bloody draft cards
October 30	Indiana U., Bloomington	40	unreported	Protest Dow recruitment
November 1	Stanford U. . Palo Alto, Calif.	110	SDS	Protest Dow recruitment

Date	Location	Number	Organizations	Action
November 3	U. of Iowa, Iowa City	n.a.	unreported	Protest Marine recruiter (demonstrators splash own blood collected in paper cups and present petition signed in blood)
November 17	Cornell U.	200	unreported	Attempt to prevent 2 US Marines from recruiting on campus
November 21	San Jose State, San Jose	500	unreported	Protest Dow recruitment (defying Reagan warning)
November 28	Federal Office Bldg, Cleveland	100	unreported	Block entrance
November 29	New York U.	200	unreported	Prevent Dow recruitment
December 4	Induction Center, Cincinnati	n.a.	WRL, WSP, Communist Party, Resistance, DuBois Club, Workshop in Nonviolence	Sit-in during Stop the Draft Week (draft cards dipped in blood and turned in)
December 7	Induction Center, New Haven, Conn.	300	same as above	Block entrance
December 18	Induction Center, Oakland	750	same as above	Block entrance
December 19	Induction Center, Oakland	750	same as above	Block entrance
1968:				
January 24	Ohio State U., Columbus	200	unreported	Sit-in to protest Marine Corps recruiters (debate with recruiters)
February 6	U. of Maine, Orono	30	unreported	Protest against Dow (prevented by police from doing anything)

TABLE II—Continued

DATE (1966)	PLACE	SIZE	ORGANIZATIONAL SPONSORSHIP	TACTICS
February 11	Boston	400	unreported	Four day fast by college students
February 14	Amherst College, Amherst, Mass.	350	unreported	Protest against Dow and Chase Bank (napalm effigy burned, napalm valentine)
February 14	Washington U.	60	SDS	Protest Dow interviews (which are postponed)
February 27	Iona College, New Rochelle, N.Y.	150	unreported	Protest against Dow
April 8	New York City	n.a.	Concerned Clergy	Fast (3 days)
May 18	New York City	400	Coalition for an Anti-Imperialist March	March (no permit; defy police by taking hide-and-seek route through lower East Side)
May 28	Dow Chemical, NYC	75	unreported	Picket
May 30	New York City	n.a.	Veterans and Reservists	Protest the war (Memorial Day)
September 1-3	Berkeley	500	Black Panthers, SDS, International Socialist Association, Young Socialist Alliance, Peace and Freedom Party	Demonstrate to support Chicago Convention anti-war demonstrators (attempt to turn two blocks of Telegraph Avenue into pedestrian mall)

TABLE III: VIOLENCE IN ANTI-WAR DEMONSTRATIONS BY 1000 OR MORE PERSONS

DATE & PLACE	SIZE	NO. POLICE & NATIONAL GUARDSMEN	MINOR INCIDENTS	MAJOR INCIDENTS	ARRESTED	INJURED
1965:						
October 16 New York City	10,000	1,000	Eggs, paint and tomatoes thrown; 1,000 Young Americans for Freedom (YAF) and National Renaissance Party (NRP) counter-demonstrate		4 counter-demonstrators	1 policeman (broken leg)
October 16 Berkeley	3,000	local police only	6 Hell's Angels attack marchers		6 counter-demonstrators	
November 6 Union Square, NYC	1,500	n.a.	60 counterdemon-strate; cards drenched by fire extinguisher		1 heckler	
November 27 Washington, D.C.	15,000-35,000	n.a.	100 Nazis counter-demonstrate; Nazis attempt to tear down unauthorized VC flags; bus drivers boycott, refuse to bring marchers to Washington		18, for disorderly conduct	
1966:						
March 26 New York City	20,000-25,000	750	NLF flag hassles; jeering and egg throwing		7, over NLF flags	
April 16 Times Square	4,400	400	40 American Patriots for Freedom counter-demonstrate; scuffles			

TABLE III—Continued

DATE & PLACE	SIZE	NO. POLICE, GUARDSMEN	MINOR INCIDENTS	MAJOR INCIDENTS	ARRESTED	INJURED
1967:						
April 15 New York City	100,000-125,000	n.a.	Jeering, paint and egg throwing; several scuffles		5, on disorderly conduct	
October 17 Oakland	3,000	n.a.	Police attack newsmen	Police stop the rioting with clubs and chemical sprays	20	
October 18 Madison	1,000	n.a.		Riot after police called in; some buildings damaged		70 students
October 19 Brooklyn	1,000	200		Violent clash with police	40 students and faculty	
October 20 Oakland	6,500	1,000		Police club 20 demonstrators		
October 21-22 Pentagon	55,000-150,000	2,500 U.S. Army; 2,500 held on reserve		Riot, with Army troops and club-wielding marshals; steps of Pentagon bloodied	686 (580 convicted)	13 U.S. marshals, 24 demonstrators, 10 soldiers
November 14 New York City	3,000	n.a.		Violence after more marchers prevented from gathering; militant minority stops traffic, hurls bags of cattle blood, stones, bottles, bricks at police.	40	Many demonstrators, 5 police
November 20 San Jose	2,000	50		Demonstrators attacked by police after refusal to disperse; tear gas and clubs used		5

December 4-8 New York City	25,000	City's entire police department mobilized on active or standby duty (28,000)		Repeated police-demonstrator counters; violent clashes	5th—264 6th—none 7th—300 8th—140	
1968:						
April 23 Oakland	2,000	300	Confiscation of truck loaded with sound equipment		at least 10	
April 26 800 campuses	200,000	n.a.	Rocks, eggs, epithets		8	3, by counter-demonstrators
April 27 New York City	87,000-100,000	n.a.	Scuffles		160, mostly for disorderly conduct	
April 30-May 21 New York City	10,000	250	Damage into the thousands of dollars; some burning of manuscripts and confiscation of papers	One month of turmoil, including suspension of school term; student occupation of 5 buildings; heavy police violence	911	216
August 28 Chicago	9,000-14,000	6,000		2 days of heavy rioting; rifle butts, bayonets, tear gas, clubs used— both at the hotel sites and in convention headquarters	583-600, for disorderly conduct	250 demonstrators, 83 policemen, 14 newsmen

TABLE IV: VIOLENCE IN ANTI-WAR DEMONSTRATIONS BY FEWER THAN 1000 PERSONS

DATE & PLACE	SIZE	NO. POLICE & NATIONAL GUARDSMEN	MINOR INCIDENTS	MAJOR INCIDENTS	ARRESTED	INJURED
1965:						
May 15 New York City	250	n.a.	Heckling, threats		29, for halting Armed Forces Day parade	
August 9 Washington, D.C.	800	n.a.	Red paint thrown on marchers		350 (sentences up to 30 days; fines up to $50)	
August 12 Oakland	300	n.a.			2	4
October 15 Ann Arbor	200	n.a.	American flag stamped on		38 (draft ex- emptions lifted)	
1966:						
March 25 Ann Arbor	200	n.a.	Scuffles with counter- demonstrators		3, for dis- orderly con- duct	
March 26 Boston	700	n.a.	Egg throwing; harassment by cyclists		11	
March 31 Boston	11	n.a.	50-75 counterdemon- strators clash with demonstrators			
April 6 Boston	300	150	Eggs thrown		1 counter- demonstrator	
May 21 New York City	300	n.a.	Eggs thrown		50 from Workshop, on disorderly conduct, re- sisting arrest	

August 17-18 Atlanta	20	n.a.		12 (leader sentenced to 120 days, no jury)	Several policemen
November 7 Harvard U.	100	n.a.	Fights with 100 counterdemonstrators; 25 demonstrators throw themselves under McNamara's car	1	
1967:					
September 20 Washington	500	n.a.	Women fight police as attempt to break through police lines	3	
October 16 Oakland	n.a.	n.a.		125	
October 19 Chicago	n.a.	n.a.	Attempt to break into induction center	18	
October 26 Oberlin College	n.a.	n.a.	Surround car of Navy recruiter		
1968:					
September 1-3 Berkeley	500	Mobilization of total Berkeley police force	Bombing of water main and damage to building under construction	30	40 demonstrators, 5 policemen

REFERENCES

Boulding, Kenneth E. 1965. "Reflections on Protest." *Bulletin of the Atomic Scientists* 21 (October): 18-20.

Chain, Steve, et al. 1968. "Telegraph Avenue in Berkeley: After the Barricades, Let the People Decide." *Ramparts* 7 (August 24).

Cressey, Donald R., and Elg Elgesem. 1968. "The Police and the Administration of Justice." *Aspects of Social Control in Welfare States*, ed. Nils Christie. London: Tavistock Publications.

Dellinger, David. 1967a. Quoted in *The New York Times* (November 16).

———. 1967b. "Resistance: Vietnam and America." *Liberation* 12 (November): 3-7.

———. 1968. Quoted in *The New York Times* (April 22).

Fishman, Jacob R., and Fredric Solomon. 1964. "Youth and Peace: A Psychosocial Study of Student Peace Demonstrators in Washington, D.C." *Journal of Social Issues* 20 (October): 54-73.

Flacks, Richard. 1967. "The Liberated Generation: An Exploration of the Roots of Student Protest." *Journal of Social Issues* 23 (July): 52-75.

Gross, Feliks. 1958. *The Seizure of Power*. New York: Philosophical Library.

Heaps, Willard A. 1966. *Riots, U.S.A.—1765-1965*. New York: Seabury Press.

Hilsman, Roger. 1962. "Internal War: The New Communist Tactic." *Modern Guerrilla Warfare*, ed. Franklin M. Osanka. New York: The Free Press of Glencoe, 452-463.

Horowitz, Irving Louis. 1964. "Noneconomic Factors in the Institutionalization of the Cold War." *The Annals of the American Academy of Political and Social Science* 351 (January): 110-120.

———. 1968. *Radicalism and the Revolt against Reason*, 2nd ed. Carbondale: Southern Illinois University Press.

Keniston, Kenneth. 1968a. *Young Radicals: Notes on Committed Youth*. New York: Harcourt, Brace & World.

———. 1968b. "Youth, Change and Violence." *The American Scholar* 37 (Spring): 227-245.

Kifner, John. 1968. "Protestors Meet in Small Groups." *The New York Times* (August 28).

Lader, Lawrence. 1959. "New York's Bloodiest Week." *American Heritage* 10 (June): 44-49, 95-98.

Little, Arthur D., Inc. 1965. *Outlook for Defense Programs— 1965-1972.* Privately printed.

Luce, Phillip A. 1966. *The New Left.* New York: McKay Publishers.

Lynd, Staughton (ed.). 1966. *Nonviolence in America: A Documentary History.* Indianapolis: The Bobbs-Merrill Co., Inc.

———. 1968a. "Radical Politics and Nonviolent Revolution." *Radical Perspectives on Social Problems,* ed. Frank Lindenfeld. New York: The Macmillan Co.

———. 1968b. *Intellectual Origins of American Radicalism.* New York: Pantheon Books.

Mailer, Norman. 1968. "The Steps of the Pentagon." *Harper's Magazine* 236 (March).

Marx, Gary T. 1967. *Protest and Prejudice: A Study of Belief in the Black Community.* New York: Harper & Row.

Menashe, Louis, and Ronald Radosh. 1967. *Teach-Ins: USA—Reports, Opinions, Documents.* New York: Frederick A. Praeger, Publishers.

Milgram, Stanley. 1963. "Behavioral Study of Obedience." *Journal of Abnormal and Social Psychology* 67 (October): 371-387.

———. 1965. "Some Conditions of Obedience and Disobedience to Authority." *Human Relations* 18 (February): 57-75.

Millis, Walter. 1956. *Arms and Men: A Study in American Military History.* New York: Putnam.

Moore, Barrington, Jr. 1968. "Thoughts on Violence and Democracy." *Proceedings of the Academy of Political Science* 29 (July): 1-12 (special issue on urban riots).

Morse, Stanley J., and Stanton Pearlman. 1968. "Nationalism, Political Protest and the Concept of National Role: A Preliminary Report on an Empirical Study of Anti-War Demonstrators." Unpublished study, University of Michigan.

Oppenheimer, Martin. 1968. "Para-Military Activities in Urban Areas." Unpublished paper, Vassar College.

Peck, Sidney M. 1967. "Notes on Strategy and Tactics; The Movement Against the War." *New Politics* 6 (Fall): 42-53.

Rainwater, Lee. 1968. "The American Working Class and Lower Class: An American Success and Failure." *Anthropological Backgrounds of Adult Education,* ed. Sol Tax et al. Boston: Center for the Study of Liberal Education for Adults at Boston University.

Shipler, David K. 1968. "Pacifists at Connecticut Farm Consider Leaving After Minutemen's Attack." *The New York Times* (August 26).

Smith, Bruce L. R. 1968. "The Politics of Protest: How Effective Is Violence?" *Proceedings of the Academy of Political Science* 29 (July): 113-130 (special issue on urban riots).

Weidenbaum, Murray L. 1967. *Impact of Vietnam War on the American Economy*. Washington, D.C.: Georgetown University (The Center for Strategic Studies).

Wofford, Harris, Jr. 1968. "Which Is the Danger: Civil Disobedience or Undue Obedience?" Address to the 91st Annual Meeting of The American Bar Association, August 6, 1968 (mimeographed).

Young Americans for Freedom (YAF). 1965. "Red Diaper Babies." *The New Guard* (September): 6-12.

NAME INDEX

173

Rusk, Dean, 15

Schaff, Adam, 90
Seale, Bobby, 102
Skolnick, Jerome H., 121, 124-6, 128-9, 131-4, 138-9, 141-2
Smith, Bruce L. R., 62
Sorel, George, 84, 86, 89-92, 94-8, 100-1
Spock, Benjamin, 56

Spooner, Lysander, 18
Stalin, Joseph, 117

Talmon, Jacob, 85
Thoreau, Henry David, 18, 138
Tolstoy, Leo, 33
Trotsky, Leon, 94

Wallace, George, 117
Wofford, Harris, 118

SUBJECT INDEX